GETTING PUBLISHED IN EDUCATION JOURNALS

GETTING PUBLISHED IN EDUCATION JOURNALS

by

ROBERT J. SILVERMAN

Professor of Education
The Ohio State University
Columbus, Ohio

CHARLES C THOMAS • PUBLISHER

Springfield • Illinois • U.S.A.

Published and Distributed Throughout the World by
CHARLES C THOMAS • PUBLISHER
2600 South First Street
Springfield, Illinois 62717, U.S.A.

© *1982 by* CHARLES C THOMAS • PUBLISHER
ISBN 0-398-04622-0
Library of Congress Catalog Card Number: 81-14349

*With THOMAS BOOKS careful attention is given to all details of
manufacturing and design. It is the Publisher's desire to present books that are
satisfactory as to their physical qualities and artistic possibilities and
appropriate for their particular use. THOMAS BOOKS will be true to those
laws of quality that assure a good name and good will.*

Library of Congress Cataloging in Publication Data

Silverman, Robert J. (Robert Jay), 1940-
    Getting published in education journals.

    Bibliography: p.
    Includes index.
    1. Education—Authorship. 2. Research.
3. Report writing. I. Title.
LB2369.S54   070.5'2   81-14349
ISBM 0-398-04622-0   AACR2

Printed in the United States of America
AFG - RX - 1

PREFACE

Graduate programs and professional experiences in education have prepared and stimulated educators to develop manuscripts for journal publication. This book has been written to assist the reader in placing his or her manuscript in an appropriate journal in the field.

The advice presented here is based on an in-depth examination of the variety of journal types in education and on my experiences in publishing and my research on the behavior of education journal editors.

As an editor who, with his colleagues, "fails to use" many submitted manuscripts, I am of the opinion that authors have limited understanding of the manuscript submission process and the way in which papers are treated following their receipt. This lack of knowledge appears to be a major cause of the high rejection rate.

There are few professional interests that are as important as publishing and that are as much informed by folk wisdom. This book challenges some of the myths and aphorisms in an attempt to empower the reader to become more successful as an author of journal articles.

ABOUT THE AUTHOR

Robert J. Silverman is Professor of Education at the Ohio State University. Since 1970 he has served as editor of the *Journal of Higher Education*, published by the Ohio State University Press.

He serves as an advisor to the publishing programs of national associations, and with the support of the National Institute of Education, he recently developed seminar-workshops for women and minority graduate-level faculty in the area of writing for funding and publication. He is currently chairperson of the Council of Editors of Postsecondary Journals.

ACKNOWLEDGMENTS

I am indebted to many editors who have shared information about their professional activities and through whom I have been able to expand my understanding of journal publishing.

In addition, I am grateful for early career support from Arliss L. Roaden, through whose offices I had the opportunity to become an editor. The editorial boards, referees, authors, and readers of the *Journal of Higher Education* have taught me much about "knowledge creation and dissemination."

The book has benefited greatly from the careful and caring editing of Rich Rose, a colleague at the Ohio state University Press. The near illegible manuscript was typed, miraculously, by Kim Hall. *Viewpoints in Teaching and Learning* has kindly allowed me to reproduce tables from my paper that appeared in their pages.

I dedicate this book to Maxine, my wife, who creates the conditions for growth in those whose lives she touches.

CONTENTS

GETTING PUBLISHED IN
EDUCATION JOURNALS

Part I
WHERE SHOULD
I SUBMIT THIS PAPER?

There are few more gratifying experiences than having one's manuscript accepted for publication by a journal whose readership will appreciate the contribution.

Achieving acceptance of one's work is not a matter of chance or knowing the "right people." Manuscript acceptance is enhanced if authors make good diagnoses both of their work and of journal interests.

Chapter 1 will provide the reader with ways to consider his or her work; Chapter 2 will outline journal types in education.

Chapter 1
DIAGNOSING YOUR APPROACH TO KNOWLEDGE IN EDUCATION

Success in disseminating education knowledge has its origin not only in the development of quality material but also in the correct placement of the finished work with a publisher. This book will not recommend a particular way of doing research, or advocate certain forms of inquiry, or even propose a method of developing a manuscript from idea to finished product, but it will recommend strategic factors for authors to consider in diagnosing their work so that they will be better able to publish in journals of interest.

There are countless ways in which authors can consider the place of their manuscripts in the range of education journals that serve the field. The following two approaches have partial—secondary or tertiary—importance, but for some they hold primary importance and thereby create unnecessary problems.

PITFALL ONE: DISCIPLINARY PATTERNS

It is common for persons in education to stress their orientation toward those social and behavioral sciences that typically provide the theoretical and methodological foundations of their inquiries. However, strong disciplinary identification, though fostered by educational curricula, in my view, does not enhance publishing opportunities in either disciplinary journals or education journals that are grounded in the social and behavioral sciences.

In the case of the social and behavioral sciences, disciplinary journals' primary constituents are members of discrete intellectual communities. An author in education who is also a marginal member of a disciplinary field might believe he or she will be legitimized by being published with, say, "real" economists or psychologists. However, it is unlikely that one will. It should be recognized, initially, that the rejection rate in the behavioral and social science journals is enormously high; it commonly reaches

90 percent. Scholars who study the dissemination of knowledge—and readers of editors' reports in disciplinary newsletters—are familiar with the rates in their fields. It is most difficult for disciplinarians to be published in their own journals, even though most know, or think they know, how to communicate as a member of an academic tribe.

One very significant reason for the differential publishing success of scholars within the social and behavioral sciences is the working of what sociologists of science call "particularistic" (as opposed to "universalistic") factors in the decision-making process. That is, editors and referees of manuscripts for journals in the social and behavioral sciences often respond to manuscripts, even when they lack author or institutional labels, on the basis of their disposition toward the kinds of questions raised and the methods used to answer them. It has been demonstrated time and again that these gatekeepers are parochial in their judgments; for example, they accept a disproportionate number of manuscripts written by persons who participated in the same Ph.D. program as they did. Thus, Crane (1972) clearly suggests that members of "invisible colleges," persons who share a specific and delimited intellectual heritage, are likely to be accepted for publication by their peers regardless of the quality of their work. We in education are not members of the invisible colleges within the social and behavioral sciences. Even though we may ask questions and use methods agreed upon by members of a broad field, the probability of being published in a specific journal with the unavoidable cognitive biases of its gatekeeper is low indeed and, in my opinion, hardly worth the effort.

In addition to the particularistic biases of editors and referees, grounded in common professional socialization experience, educators, especially those in or preparing for a faculty role, should understand "education" as a field and how it differs from others that may claim a cognitive allegiance. It is only when we are better aware of such differences that we can be more effective in using disciplinary material in ways appropriate for education journals.

To assist in considering field differences, I employ the heuristic ideas of Anthony Biglan (1973a, b) and those scholars (Smart and Elton, 1975; Smart and McLaughlin, 1978) who have replicated and built on his work. Based on actual faculty activities in various fields of study, Biglan identified three differentiating dimensions among the universe of disciplines and fields of study. Some fields are (a) hard/soft, a dimension based on the availability and focusing power of a particular paradigm that informs scholars about what questions need to be raised and in what ways they might be answered; (b) pure/applied, a dimension that asks which is more important, the internal logic or external value of a body of knowledge; and (c) life/nonlife, a dimension that labels the object of scholarship as organic or nonorganic.

Biglan's ideas have been used to examine the goals of academic departments as well as the behavior of students and faculty, including professional communication patterns, in fields differentiated by these dimensions. For example, there is some evidence that published articles have a longer history in the harder, purer fields than in the social and behavioral sciences. Initially refereed for conference use, and subsequently critiqued at the time of presentation, the published manuscript has often been examined critically and substantially revised within a "friendly" colleague network before submission to a journal.

In the pure, soft, and nonlife humanities, such as English, the published work often has a substantial history with the author, who may have written and thought about a delimited area for many years. Growth is measured more by increased wisdom than by substantial modification to either interests or questions raised. Such fields ripen under the skin; others, such as education, grow on top. It should also be noted that scholars play different roles in the various fields according to rank or career age. In some the senior scholar may write the manuscript, and in others it may be the younger faculty member (Lewis, 1975).

Suffice it to say that all fields not only have special theoretical commitments but also commitments informed by particular patterns of behavior. Education scholars attempting to publish in the social and behavioral sciences must have an understanding of the normative posture of the fields they are attempting to influence. Thus, in addition to the particularistic criteria that keep educators out, they infrequently publish in the disciplines that inform their view of education because they do not think and act as members of specific academic fields.

At this point, I should note that education journals are not particularly interested in pursuing questions that the disciplines believe are important. The fields do have a part to play in the development of knowledge disseminated in education journals, but considering oneself a *psychologist* or *sociologist* of education is not an attitude that will enhance one's publishing success.

PITFALL TWO: TOPICAL AND PROFESSIONAL PATTERNS

Journal editors are constantly confronted by authors who want to know the topics that are currently "hot". Alternatively, writers promise submission on a specific topic about which the editor is requested to comment. Although these initiatives are usually fashioned in letters and telephone conversations, they also occur in conference settings—especially at cocktail parties—in which the publicness of the requested reaction is an enemy of its validity. Certainly, education journals respond to topical issues in the field; however, the inherent difficulties in overemphasizing this approach call its value into question. Responding to a "hot" topic is likely to be unproductive for a number of reasons and on a number of levels.

It is unlikely that an author will have a polished manuscript available on a topic that is receiving its play in the field. Even if there is one "in the drawer," the author must keep in mind that the time lapse from submission to publication is often well over a year. Assuming the typical need for revision, if not a series of rejections before acceptance, the topical thrust may have changed—or expired—by the time the work is ready for publication.

On a more strategic level, it should be noted that education journals often do not follow the national agenda. As will be seen later, they typically fulfill editors' agenda, and manuscripts that are the object of their vision are frequently commissioned. Editors' meaning systems are not necessarily related to the fields' yearly infatuations. This may be the year of affirmative action or international education or competency-based education, but for the editor who is at the forefront of developing priorities, the important messages have already been written and new "years" have to be planned.

Certainly, an author might be fortunate enough, and it really is luck, to submit a manuscript that rounds out a special, topical issue of a journal, but still the chances for acceptance are lower than would be expected. Even when a journal publishes a "call for manuscripts," particularistic relationships often find their way into the editorial decision process. The editor usually must seek support from various quarters in the form of direct solicitation, and the resulting manuscripts, based as they are on prior commitments, have a more than equal opportunity.

It cannot be overemphasized that authors make the error of assuming that journals that focus on professional areas do so with an "open market" philosophy. But, at times, the misunderstanding goes deeper. As scholars who study knowledge dissemination and utilization in education know, practitioners read to serve their professional interests in their organizations. That is, they are shopping for ideas whose local implementation might enhance their posture in an organization or to find support for ideological positions taken or programs already implemented. There are, of course, other reasons for reader interest, but it seems evident that if a journal focuses on a topic, it is also concerned about the treatment the area is likely to receive. This is not the place to analyze the assumptions and values of those messages that appear in the preponderance of education journals that attend to professional issues, but the existence of latent agendas or hidden curricula should not be ignored.

In addition to understanding the vested interests of journals, authors should recognize that publications not only influence but are influenced by the power relationships in fields. They are legitimized by those authors whose papers are accepted and are honored by the relationship. But, it is the publication of the "notorious" and of forward-looking persons, and legitimized practice descriptions that many editors believe will validate the journal as worthy of attention. Although a newsstand mentality might operate more directly on journals focusing on topical and professional patterns, it is known to exist among those editors and, even more, among members of their boards, who publish traditional scholarship. A notice in the *New York Times* would not be resisted.

If an author has to ask about the vitality of a topic, it is likely that he or she is insufficiently close to current developments and would not bring honor to the journal.

The purpose of this discussion is to suggest that success in publishing one's work in education journals is not likely to be enhanced if it is directed solely by "self-orientations."

Should one's presumed strength be based on disciplinary socialization and orientation or familiarity and involvement with issues of the day or innovative professional activity, these should be considered second, not first-order foundations for manuscript development. They are the bedrock upon which the manuscript might be able to satisfy the editor, referees, and readers, but as noted, there are varieties of strengths, and it is often the brand that sells the product.

Authors must answer the question "Why am I writing this paper?" with the interests of the field, the readers, and the editor clearly in the forefront. The narcissistic tendencies with which all writers flirt must be controlled and balanced with an external orientation. Journals satisfy authors' interests indirectly by certifying their relatedness to others' priorities. It is responsiveness that is rewarded. Fortunately, this still allows many options.

WHY AM I WRITING THIS PAPER?

Although this book is designed to assist authors in publishing rather than in writing manuscripts, it should be noted that creative work, regardless of methodological sophistication or topical relevance, is difficult to place. At the very beginning of one's writing—and even earlier, when foci and methodologies are being considered—it is wise to give serious thought to the implications of one's choices for publishing the manuscript. Clearly, separating the creative aspects of one's scholarship from the more instrumental aspect of placement of the product is not productive. One ought to have a readership in mind from the very beginning. As we will learn in Chapter 2, an author's diagnosis of his or her motives for writing a paper will suggest classes or types of journals that are likely to be receptive to the work.

Motivators

Various rationales for writing may co-exist, but it is likely that one will be dominant.

To Add to Existing Knowledge

Most of the empirical educational literature is built upon the work of others. Authors identify theories, instruments, and designs in order to pursue lines of reasoning within established frameworks.

It is common in the "harder" fields for schools of thought to emerge, each with its adherents and often with its own publications and conferences. Powerful research frameworks demanding the attention of large numbers of scholars are rarer in education. It is not unusual, however, to notice titles that suggest that authors are developing heuristic paradigms that they hope will capture the attention of other scholars. At times, educational associations, perceiving the field as pre-paradigmatic, outline major research programs which are not only designed to contribute to an understanding of a domain, such as "the deanship," but also to define the research direction for the field, such as educational administration. In brief, contributing to a larger scholarship effort is frequently the rationale for the development of one's work.

Scholars in the sociology of science would argue that the traditional empirical scholarship in education be labelled "analytic science," and as such it shows certain features. Mitroff and Kilmann note that the basic tenet of analytic science is that "precision, accuracy and reliability necessarily serve the ultimate aim of scientific knowledge, which is unambiguous theoretical or empirical knowledge" (1978, p. 33). Certainty and consensus are paramount. "A scientific observation is judged valid, reliable, or certain if two or more 'competent' observers in different places at different times can agree on what they have observed" (1978, p. 35).

Research quality, as traditionally defined and examined through attention to sophistication of statistics, tightness of design, appropriateness of sampling procedures, and the like, is critical. At the same time, but of less significance, manuscripts designed as contributions to knowledge often are expected to address and solve problems in the field. Frankly, it is rare for scholars, as analytical scientists, to pay much attention to the value of their work for practitioners. The assumption seems to be, "If it is quality scholarship, it should be used to deal with the issue it addresses. Good decisions rest on valid and reliable data."

There is a growing literature in the sociology of knowledge application that successfully goes behind the myths to assess how analytic science actually is used in practice settings: the factors endemic to the research, the practice setting, and the linkage elements that impede or facilitate the use of scientific work. One of the major findings in this literature is captured by Weiss, who believes that research "provides an underlying set of ideas, models of the interaction of people, conditions, and events, which enter into our images of how the world works" (1980a, p. 397). Some practitioners read to continue their formal education, others do so ritualistically, some to rethink assumptions or to support their presuppositions or to embellish their arguments. It is clearly unreasonable to believe that any one study has an impact on practice. In Weiss's terms, there is "knowledge creep" (1980a), and one's work is likely to add its value to the growing literature.

A growing body of knowledge may have an incremental impact not only because of its internal structure, which is frequently more important than its external value, but also because of the way it is read. Wilson, writing about generic types of knowledge sources, suggests that most science provides a potential rather than an actual supply of information (1977, p. 37). It is a "reserve system," used irregularly or not at all but still known to be available for use. Accessing information through retrieval systems, practitioners are likely to search when a problem or issue is relevant; they do not read an article upon its publication.

There is evidence that empirical material is not widely read by academics or by practitioners. We value its publication and spend huge sums on storing it. It is proper that the new "sociology of science use" is growing, for it will help direct us in producing work that does more than sit on a computer tape or a yellowing page.

To Develop Understanding

There are at least two major approaches taken by education authors whose basic motive is to develop reader understanding: literature review and conceptual scholarship. The first is a special critical use of the analytic literature, and the second is a less fettered creative venture.

First, it is obvious that knowledge is growing rapidly, that the units of analysis (variables) are growing smaller, and that the contingencies operating in the experimental situation limit generalizability. Actual usefulness of research is more likely to be the result of readers' understanding of a corpus of knowledge rather than one or more individual studies.

Given the narrowed focus of studies and readers' need for integrated understanding, authors and editors are becoming more interested in reviews of literature. Authors can contribute to understanding through creative, comprehensive, and critical analyses of existing analytic scholarship—examining empirical gaps as well as the meaning and value of the literature. There is a growing body of knowledge available to assist authors in developing integrations and meta-analyses of published studies. As forms, they have a stronger tradition in the hard sciences than in the social and behavioral areas or in education. Yet, they do exist and will increase in importance.

Conceptual scholarship is not tied to a current line of reasoning or the existing literature in a delimited domain; it is freer and more intuitive in style. Oliver Wendell Homes, Jr., noted that "there are one story intellects, two story intellects and three story intellects with skylights. Three story men idealize, imagine, predict. Their best illumination comes from above through the skylight" (Mueller, 1980, p. 26). Conceptual scholarship, produced by three story people, enhances understanding.

As Mitroff and Kilmann suggest, persons who do this work "seek out or produce multiple explanations for any phenomenon" (1978, p. 54). They are "directed not toward the quest for and resolution of conflict but toward the toleration, proliferation, and enjoyment of ambiguity and of multiple ways of viewing the world" (1978, p. 67).

Conceptual theory is speculative, creative, often attempting to develop new frameworks for describing or prescribing behavior, combining playfulness and reason while asking and answering interesting questions. Authors who attempt to develop understanding engage in lateral thinking, plumbing and probing the meaning and possibilities of ideas. They have to overcome the difficulties of confronting readers who may think in more linear or hierarchical patterns. One might label an accomplished author, in this mode, "erudite" or "learned," and the analytic colleague "sophisticated."

Using Nisbet and Broadstreet's term, the conceptualist, through an "epistemological spark," must cross into the cognitive world of the reader, introducing new concepts and complexities (1980).

An author's awareness of the reader's social setting, likely unfamiliarity with nonhierarchical problem finding and solving, and skepticism of untested propositions suggests the need for such a scholar to proceed with empathy and humility at the same time he or she develops rich, connotative work.

Argyris and Schön (1974) differentiated between espoused theories, those we say we use, and theories-in-use, those which we actually use. To the degree that conceptualists' espoused theories are connected with readers' theories-in-use, they will be successful in bringing their ideas to everyday professional behavior.

To Improve the Effectiveness of Professional Systems

"Theory into practice" is a well-worn phrase whose realization many scholars assume is based on practitioners' "correct attitude" toward the products of research and theory. If only it were so easy. The linkage between the cognitive worlds of the idea advocate and the administrator or teacher is problematic. It can be facilitated by a variety of factors, including the topical focus, the methods of scholarly work, and the manner in which the manuscript is written.

It is instructive to examine the titles and abstracts of papers appearing in education journals. Certain journals publish manuscripts whose legitimization is based on research questions and methods that maintain continuity in a line of research. Other publications focus more directly on discrete practice areas using manuscripts whose elements are pieced together, concatenated from a number of disciplines. The following article titles suggest the differences: "Aptitude Treatment Interactions in an Experiment of Teacher Effectiveness" and "Alternatives to Student Ratings of College Teaching." The second title is more organic and less linear.

Nagi and Corwin note, "The hierarchical model is better suited for codifying the principles of developed fields; the basic premises and axioms in such theories are highly abstract. . . .When concatenated theories are focused on social and technical problems, the yield is applicable knowledge (1972, p. 8). The differences between the hierarchical and organic models are more than skin deep; they reflect the authors' "master": the question or the practice-oriented reader. It is clear that the development of knowledge designed to improve the effectiveness of professional systems is intrinsically different from that which has no strong commitment beyond itself.

Many scholars of "knowledge creation" have identified the differences between the two approaches and have given them connotative labels. Mitroff and Kilmann discriminate between "analytical science" and "conceptual humanism." The latter is oriented "not (to) how science, methodology, and experimentation can serve some abstract theoretical concepts of truth per se but how they can further humanity as a whole" (1978, p. 78). Chris Argyris (1970) differentiates between rigorous and organic science, the latter oriented to the development of useful information having behavioral, not necessarily statistical, significance. In fact, Argyris suggests that authors ought to do research on manipulable variables, using methodologies that respect the information-processing abilities of readers, and that research should stand up to noise in the system (1972).

In a similar vein, Evered and Susman, note the bias of "action research" toward "understanding" rather than explanation, making things happen rather than predicting things, imaginative leaps and conjectures rather than contemplation (1978). In addition to methodological prescriptions, there exists a vital philosophical literature examining approaches to responsible scholarship that focuses on the world of everyday behavior.

If such work is topical and situational, so the literature also supports greater collaboration between the author and clients (not subjects) in all phases of the knowledge creation experience—from shaping major questions to the use of the research. There are clear value implications to the author-practitioner relationship and pragmatic ones as well. Research is likely to be used, says Rothman, if organizational participants are actively involved in all phases of the research effort (1980). Rothman highlights the value of simplicity in language and statistical presentation, concreteness, action orientation and practical relearning, and responsiveness to the enlightened self-interest of the reader.

Improvement of the effectiveness of professional systems is not an element in the potential value of any and all knowledge. It will be a primary orientation of an author's work to the degree that methods of scholarship and elements of the written product explicitly support such a direction.

To Gain Personal Insight

Certainly, the forms of scholarship noted above add to our insight into the functioning of both educational systems and organizational members as role occupants. The bulk of the educational literature that examines persons as professionals regards classes, such as students, teachers, guidance counselors, or departmental chairpersons. However, authors may focus on a single person and through such direct attention may attempt to understand, deeply and holistically, other persons and ultimately, oneself. Mitroff and Kilmann call such scholarship "personal humanism," and they posit that "no amount of quantitative sophistication or theoretical generalization can substitute for the physical presence of a concerned, caring, human observer and the interaction that takes place between observer and observed" (1978, p. 97).

This is more than, and different from, biography. Authors share in the existential dilemmas, confront the process of life, and share an intimacy that, with readers, might allow all "participants" to review their choices, to refresh the inner dialogue, to grow. Authors with such an orientation allow readers to deepen their intimacy with themselves by encountering the personhoods of authors and subjects.

Obviously, traditional educational methodologies have no bearing here. In fact, Mitroff and Kilmann believe that the norms that inform such scholarships are counter to the norms of the analytical scientist (1978, pp. 102-3). It may be that those whose intellectual foundations are in the humanities or psychiatry will find this form of educational inquiry more appealing than does the majority of educators trained in more conventional education curricula. Nonetheless, charting and understanding existential concerns in order to enhance our humanity and to understand the challenges to humanism from group, organizational, and social system dynamics is an approach to scholarship that manifests a concrete caring. As examples in the current literature, one finds manuscripts that take us into the life of a female faculty member confronting the meaning of her gender in her and other's eyes; an undergraduate commuter who, practically illiterate and without purpose, confronts a massive university bureaucracy whose policies, as they pertain to him, he does not begin to understand; a scholar who, unable to gain academic employment, likens his feelings to what he believes is the journey toward death.

The discovery of one life is often more powerful to the reader than a paper whose sampling is rigorous and whose data pertain to large populations. Whether readers have the courage to act on such feelings is the challenge with which most are left.

To Increase Professional Awareness and Understanding of Issues

Practitioners confront an endless procession of immediate issues that relate to their roles in educational organizations. Authors believe they can assist the exercise of leadership through problem solving by raising awareness of issues and deepening reader understanding of their parameters.

Authors may elucidate issues by addressing them in different educational environments through the use of case studies that describe the positive and negative consequences of different resolutions. They may suggest what issues should have priority in relation to contemporary pragmatic, political, or value contexts. Respected spolespersons are often invited to comment on critical concerns and to suggest needed professional directions. Authors often here have solutions looking for problems. And editors plan special issues whose attractiveness rests not on the voice of a single writer but on the sustained focus a topical issue receives.

Readers, in fact, respond well to both of the latter approaches to publishing—to the one to determine what the important people think and to the other to provide integration in a professional world that allows for precious little focus. Whether the issue be accreditation, access, or acceleration (to note only a few issues that begin with "acc"), readers can become more sensitive to their current situations, the actors who are in the forefront in dealing with certain problems, and their treatment elsewhere. In this sense, authors can provide a monitoring function (Wilson, 1977, p. 37) for the reader, somewhat like the reserve function more scholarly papers serve.

Commitment and intimate familarity often mark the successfully written manuscript whose origin is not in an external knowledge base and whose persuasive power does not rest on exciting and sophisticated methodology. The questions are "Is the problem a real and significant one, and does the author have the reasoning power, understanding, or battle scars that will attract reader attention?" Writers must prove themselves to readers, if not on the basis of position, say, as a foundation or government executive, then on their groundedness, their "no-nonsense" approach, with short-run utility.

As might be evident, a good deal of the literature devoted to increasing professional understanding either is commissioned by the editor or appears first in such contexts as a conference program or a section of a newly published book. The average author, then, is competing not only with other unsolicited work but with those who have easier access to the page. We will discuss the implications of this competitive framework later.

To Support Professional Directions

Advocacy is the final motivation to be considered. Although all authors advocate, to some degree, by simply giving attention to topics or issues and using particular methods, all informed by various values, an author's primary intent may be to persuade the reader to take a position on a professional matter.

Editors' mailboxes are stuffed with manuscripts whose principal verbs are "should," "ought," and "might." Attempts to persuade the reader often spring from perspectives and experiences that the authors believe address the issues so very successfully that they should provide the frameworks for optimal change elsewhere.

Active lobbying is not the sole route available to authors who want their opinions to count. Educators who are providing leadership through innovative practice are frequently persuaded by colleagues or editors to describe their work with the expectation that they might be emulated. Ours is an experiential field, and many who are making a difference in practice are not strongly committed to writing about their work; and even if there is a spark, they may have limited skills in writing and placing a manuscript.

Of course, advocacy is an organizational as well as an individual behavior. Witness the multitude of association newsletters and journals that focus on selected issues; campaigning often presents itself as mere information. In a culture that is as heavily narcissistic and political as ours is, it is understandable that much of the literature in our field is in the advocacy mold.

If the manuscript designed to increase professional understanding is couched in non-jargonish, simple, concrete language, so papers intending to persuade should "tell it like it is." A strong, sparse, value-laden style is the mark of such education writing.

This approach to communication in education manifests the third of Wilson's (1977, p. 37) knowledge functions: providing advice. Earlier it was noted that traditional scholarly material serves in a "reserve" capacity and that professional writing assumes a monitoring function. With this final function, we embrace the variety of values written educational materials usually have for readers. It is not that the various motivations and functions are in competition; they serve different and legitimate purposes. Manuscripts themselves must reflect these differences. For example, if persuasive literature is to serve in an advisory capacity, it must embody the characteristics we value in advisors; and this requires that we know their assumptions, values, and experiences. The advisor-authors should speak our language and, to compensate for the drawbacks of written communication, anticipate our questions to simulate a dialogue.

These, then, are the reasons that authors put pen to paper to develop manuscripts for submission to education journals: to add to existing knowledge, to develop both self and reader understanding, to improve the effectiveness of professional systems, to gain insight, to increase professional awareness and understanding of issues, and to support professional directions.

The author should treat one motivation as primary. Although there may be secondary motives, such as an intention to persuade while attempting to gain insight, the focal objective suggests norms, values, methods, and contents that are likely to be responsive to either specific readers or those who have a wide range of appetites. Many of us are interested in developing an awareness of emerging issues as well as deepening our understanding of a research problem. One article cannot adequately satisfy both demands. Implicity, readers read for different reasons. Manuscripts are more likely to be successful if they adequately address the motivations shared with the audiences.

There is another more immediate reason to ask the question "Why am I writing this paper?" Education journals are differentially responsive to manuscripts with various motives. Knowing the purpose of the manuscript is critical in its placement.

Chapter 2
TYPES OF EDUCATION JOURNALS

Journals expire, but more are born—to contribute to what Warren Bennis identified as "information-overload anxiety" for which "the only promising [cure]. . .is the total collapse of the U.S. Postal Service" (1977, p. 159). Most of us, however, have a strong interest in contributing to the disease.

There are hundreds of journals in education. They come in different colors, sizes, and shapes, have various foci, and are published by a variety of sponsors, including university presses, education agencies—local, state, and federal—commercial firms, and professional societies, both scholar and practitioner oriented. Authors must decide which are appropriate for their work, and they often do so with very imperfect information, unaware of the journals that are available and, specifically, of those that might have an interest in their work.

This chapter is designed to create some order out of the confusion. It will begin by critiquing some ways of thinking about education journals that have secondary value but are often mistakenly given primary significance. Next, it presents a framework for considering the placement of manuscripts on the basis of authors' writing motives.

MISTAKEN PRIORITIES

Refereed vs. Non-Refereed Journals

Promotion and tenure documents typically differentiate between refereed and non-refereed journals. What, in fact, makes a journal refereed? Is there validity to the commonly understood notion that a refereed journal is one that transmits its received manuscripts to authors' peers for review, and further that the "better" referees are those not so closely affiliated with the editor that their judgments will be influenced by the editor's proximity or status?

As a rule, no manuscript is published until it has been read and reviewed by persons in addition to the editor. Depending on the publisher and the purposes that the journals serve, the referees may be externally based scholars, possibly affiliated with the journal as members of an editorial board, or agency staff members, or practitioners who are retained to check on an article's accuracy, or even conference leaders who judge the value of papers that are to appear in published proceedings. Reaction to manuscripts coming under the purview of this variety of referees are transmitted to the editors, who make judgments regarding the papers' value to their journals. Of course, in the case of conference proceedings, the editor has the decision made by others.

It is common for two or more referees to focus on different elements of the same manuscript, regardless of the editors' specific instructions and, on the other hand, to come to different conclusions should they react to the same properties. The editor judges not only the paper but the readers' reactions.

In fact, the term "refereed" is a euphuism used by many to support the primacy of the research journal that publishes traditional investigations. The "peer reviewers" for this type of publication are typically not employed by the organization for which the editor works—as much a result of the pattern of scholar employment as an effort toward impartiality—though significant involvement by local personnel is not unknown.

The question, it would appear, is not whether a manuscript, or journal, is refereed or not. All are. Although many argue that a more valuable contribution is one that is acknowledged as such by persons who are experts in an area of inquiry or practice, there clearly are subtle political factors that enter into referees' judgments. Some find it difficult to approve a paper whose conclusions take issue with their work or with field consensus. Not only does reputation often mean bias, but those referees lacking reputation often blindly support their mentors or believe one gains renown by slinging a battery of large and small stones at the competition.

Instead of reserving our approval only for "refereed" publications, we should value those journals whose review processes are balanced, fair, and helpful to authors. Since these measures are not visible and the names and institutions appearing on the masthead are, reputations of individuals and institutions become the yardstick for review quality. One may not be able to escape this reality, but one can give it the secondary importance it deserves.

Prestigious vs. Non-Prestigious Journals

Along with the term "refereed," there is the notion of "prestige." The two are frequently used together, though they pertain to different aspects of a publication. There are a number of common indicators of a prestigious journal. It may be the primary journal in an area of inquiry, publishing the most significant contributions; it may be the only publication in a domain, or it may publish national spokespersons and speak to national agenda. It may be the publication of a national organization; it may be read by a large number of people; or its board may be drawn from a broad, high-quality base.

We all seem to know what a prestigious journal is and would rather be published in one. Some academic departments, using local or national disciplinary data, even rank journals in the field, giving different quality points to colleagues who publish in different journals. An article in a "10" is better than one in a "6," and possibly better than two in "5s."

However, education, as a field, is different from the traditional disciplines, and this has implications that create uncertainty in attempts to rank publications. Is a journal prestigious when its large number of subscribers receive the publication free as a condition of organizational membership? If education is a multiparadigmatic, multidisciplinary, topically oriented field, not evidencing clear continuity among published work, can we use the number of citations a journal garners as a measure of its prestige?

If a journal publishes highly heuristic papers that assist readers in opening new lines of thought rather than directing them to conduct a controlled experiment, or publishes practice-oriented papers whose fruits are to be found in organizational innovations, can we say they are less prestigious because the output cannot be measured? Is a narrowly focused journal whose articles are avidly read by a committed readership less prestigious than a broadly based publication receiving marginal actual use?

All things being equal, one might prefer to be published in a national rather than a regional journal, or one published by a major university press rather than by a university department, or an older journal rather than a newly created one which might not have a large library circulation. However, perceived prestige can obfuscate by getting in the way of more critical strategic and tactical considerations.

A TYPOLOGY OF EDUCATION JOURNALS

If refereeing procedures and status differentials are inappropriate guides to journal choice, what in addition to substantive focus, should an author consider? In fact, a writer ought to establish the explicit or implicit motive in a manuscript. It should suggest a journal that might have an interest in the work. There are research, scholarly, professional, and association journals in education. Each type has its own personality, and within types each journal has an editor who defines the publication somewhat atypically. We will relate motives to journal type.

The Research Journal

Historically, scientists have exhibited a passionate commitment to the development of scholarship intended to advance the state of knowledge within disciplines. Science, once outside the formal boundaries of the academy, now prospers within, as does the adjudication of the work that is being executed. The research journal, typically edited by university scholars, serves to legitimate that knowledge, and indirectly those scholars who enrich the discipline by exploring significant research questions and providing an agenda for continuing scientific work.

However, education, unlike the natural and behavioral sciences, is developmentally immature and, as such, highly dependent on the basic disciplines for its substantive foundations. Education research is grounded in theories, uses as supportive literature, and proceeds methodologically in terms that have traditions in other fields. Most popular, of course, are the psychological specialties, such as cognitive and developmental psychology, but clearly struggling for a share of journal publication are studies framed by historical, sociological, and economic theories.

Education research journals publish knowledge designed primarily to advance educational scholarship having foundations in other fields of study. Journals that examine education broadly have a multidisciplinary approach; those with a narrower focus have a multispecialty perspective. A research journal's official mission might include an interest in resolving problems or issues in the field, but it does so through the publication of analytical science which is precise, reliable, and value-free. Through such a commitment, education as a field of study will grow and mature, using more rigorous ways of knowing and developing new lines of inquiry that will spawn additional studies.

The editors of research journals, typically university professors, serve usually for periods of less than four years and spend 35 percent or less of their time managing the constant flow of manuscripts. Many, of course, have served as referees or associate editors before assuming the primary leadership role. Because of the depth of individual papers and, collectively, their breadth, as well as the limited time commitment to the role, the editor must rely on referees who are specialists in those areas represented in submitted manuscripts. They are active researchers in an area and are presumed to have an in-depth understanding of the literature and research in the field. The editor may have insight into methodological dimensions of a paper, but, except for advice offered by a specialist, he or she is unlikely to be aware of the content value of a manuscript. Frequently, even the statistical treatment of a paper is so sophisticated or based on practices in fields not frequently represented in education journals, such as mathematics or economics, that it too requires special refereeing.

It is not unusual for disciplinary or specialization factions to believe they are receiving less than their fair share of pages in the research journals. Although editors and referees in the social sciences influence, as a result of common backgrounds with authors, what is published, there have been no studies of such behavior in education. If particularistic decision making, or bias, exists, it is my belief that it is primarily oriented toward methodology rather than content, though it may be difficult to separate clearly these dimensions. Put differently, a historical question answered by way of statistical treatment is likely to have a more equal chance than if it were approached using traditional historiography. Further, as in psychology, where manuscripts with positive results, supporting a line of work, are more frequently accepted, one might posit this as another form of particularistic bias in education.

As filters maintain the purity or cleanliness of fluids, so education research journals perform the filtering function for education research. The dross is kept out of the system—it is hoped; only material that is significantly connected with previous work, related to specialists' current communities of interest, and pointed toward new research questions will find the necessary support for publication. If all editors are concerned about quality control, research journal gatekeepers seem to use the term as a battle cry, preserving the literature from type I and II errors, equating rigor with value, assuming moderate concern for readers' interest and a low concern for publishers'. There is a weak interest, if any, in communicating to nonspecialists.

Clearly, research journals contribute positively to the research enterprise by maintaining a sharp concern for reliable and valid knowledge. In an applied field the tendency to convert beliefs and myths to truth is strong indeed, and educational research serves as a necessary corrective. At the same time, as Mahoney notes (1976, p. 102), research journals contribute to some dysfunctions. He believes that their publishing biases lead to (1) "probability pyramiding"—the publication of succesful studies, suggesting a misleading reliability or consensus; (2) "research myopia"—the asking of questions that can be evaluated by the null hypothesis and allowing for statistically significant results; (3) "data hounding"—the searching for statistical procedures to yield positive results that force the transformation of data; and (4) "distortion"—the elimination of difficulties by the "rewriting [of] method[s] or hypotheses to fit [the] results."

There are research journals devoted to many education specialties as well as to the field as a whole. They not only publish research but they define its qualities. Education scholars should be aware of the impact of research journals and other journal types in shaping what knowledge is worthy of being called "knowledge".

The Scholarly Journal

If research journals serve a primary commitment to the extension of current scientific work, scholarly journals are responsive to developing understanding, improving the effectiveness of professional systems, and fostering insight.

Scholarly journals present what can be labelled "concatenated" research, scholarship focusing on problems, using theoretical, empirical, and methodological resources from a variety of domains. Additionally, there is great emphasis placed on the vitality of a manuscript, whether it is realized through its methodological, theoretical, or existential attributes. The material, optimally, should move the reader; it should force a "silent dialogue" with the material; it should suggest new ways of thinking about problems. In fact, it should raise to awareness issues that the reader begins to believe are absolutely critical; at the same time, there is room for humor, satire, paradox. Scholarly journals are very concerned about committing type III errors—publishing material that is not interesting.

Focusing scholarship on practice, this journal type serves a linking role. What is assumed to be a by-product of articles appearing in research journals here becomes a goal and, by and large, a most difficult one to reach. There is a never-ending flow of scholarship from authors who suggest implicitly or explicitly that they have successful approaches or solutions to problems in the field. They have been developed, however, with very limited interaction with practitioners for whom the material is being published. Thus, these journals, and the editors who direct them, must anticipate or assume the value of papers that ought to be useful. Of course, the location of the editor, in the academy or education agency, works to shape the editor's orientation and information needs. Interestingly, scholarly journal editors receive few letters from the field in reaction to published work. There is a tradition of research challenges appearing in the research journals, but it is the author of the scholarly journal article who receives letters. Unless the feedback is shared with the editor, this person is simultaneously at the center of a communication system and in the dark.

The field of education, as the scholarly journal defines it, should not be the product of multiple influences from other disciplines. It should be defined as orchestrated. Field development results which through the agency of the journal, provides options or alternatives to decision makers. The suggestions are likely to have long-term rather than short-term utility, may loosen up existing assumptions, and allow for alternative practices, concepts, or metaphors to take hold of practitioners' consciousness.

The editors who provide leadership, in comparison with research journal colleagues, do so for shorter or longer terms and are less likely to have had editorial experience before assuming their positions. In fact, the heuristic orientation of the publications might be supported by this staffing pattern. Vitality can spring from experimentation born from new encounters as well as from lengthy service which allows room for change. As it is less likely for these editors to serve set three-year terms, so the dynamic of the first-year orientation, second-year mastery, and third-year withdrawal may be less applicable. These editors must define, for themselves and for the field, the meaning and value of their publications. There is no three-year bell to save them from boredom or negative reader reaction.

Commitments of scholarly journal editors, in relation to their research counterparts, extend not only to a greater interest in the reader but to a closer working relationship with the publisher as well. University presses or national professional organizations are not simply patrons but agencies that realize their "official" goals through the publications themselves.

In contrast to the editorial board members of research publications, editorial board members of scholarly journals are not chosen primarily for their specialization in areas typically represented in submitted manuscripts or for their scholarly abilities. A variety of factors are at play: ability to represent the divergent interests of the readers, possession of an in-depth knowledge of the literature and research of the field, generalist orientation, involvement as administrative leaders, representation not only of schools of thought but also of minority groups and geographic regions. Editorial boards of scholarly journals are likely to decide on special issues, publishing a call for manuscripts and commissioning papers for such issues. They are likely to react to editors' ideas, suggesting policy options to make the publications more interesting and more useful.

The major problem facing scholarly journals is, paradoxically, based on their strengths. This type of publication attempts to develop synergy through the variety of purposes served by the manuscripts, the linkage it attempts to develop between scholarship and practice, and the sensibilities of the more broadly committed generalist scholars who develop policy and review papers. The results of these combined strengths, in service to the development of integration, highlights none. There is no prime beneficiary, in the narrow sense. Put differently, who cares?

The readers, as practitioners, are likely not to be contributors to the journal and may never submit a paper because of limited scholarship skills. The authors often are neither readers nor subscribers since the journal in its breadth, methodologically and topically, is not central to their narrower interests. The board members have a somewhat distant interest since their own brand of scholarship is not the journal's focus, and it is their wisdom rather than their operational advice that is solicited. The publisher, though committed to quality, has many operational interests regarding the readers, who, perhaps as members of educational organizations, need to be served in more direct ways.

The burden, or the challenge, falls on the editor to work with interests, partial and often at cross-purposes, even poorly articulated, and to develop and maintain them in providing vitality and direction. The editor shapes the work indirectly, by piecing together rather than by exercising quality control over a uniform product. This difference suggests strategies for authors, and they will be discussed in the following chapters.

The Professional Journal

The research journal's focus is provided by studies written in standard formats; the scholarly journal relies on the editor to give shape to the forces at play; the professional journal's direction is also a function of editor initiative, but an initiative based on this person's understanding of the prominent issues of the day.

Professional journals publish those manuscripts whose aim is to increase professionals' understanding, not in terms of scholarship but in terms of the everyday life of practice. The commitment is primarily to the readers' interests as perceived by the editor. There is little regard for education as a field of study, and, curiously, the commitment to the resolution of problems or issues is less consistent than that evidenced by scholarly publications. Although publisher loyalty is high, there is less of an interest in manuscript quality control and in influencing persons outside education to consider the problems that face this social institution.

Editors of professional journals develop notions based primarily on their experiences and readings, both formal and informal, of contemporary conditions. Their observations, experiences, and judgments, as well as those of persons associated with them, shape the selection and treatment of issues. Although many manuscripts are submitted by persons in the field, the unsolicited manuscript has limited opportunity for publishing consideration unless it shows freshness and high writing quality.

Much is commissioned directly from authors whose work is known, who will provide few surprises, and whose contributions promise to package well. Of course, an unsolicited manuscript may "round out an issue," but the published material by and large is created through the agency of the editor as professional generalist. Implicitly, the field does not develop through reference to other disciplines or through the editor's orchestration. Development occurs through the sponsorship of ideas and people that the editor believes should be of interest.

The staff of professional associations are frequently involved in refereeing. At times, editors hire referees to comment on manuscripts written especially for proprietary professional journals. Board members are chosen who represent the interests of the readers and who, in comparison with editors of other types of journals, are not expected to have an in-depth knowledge of the field's literature or to be specialists or scholars. They are generalists who may have positions of administrative leadership and represent a geographic region. These associates, with the editors, strive to publish work that is timely, practical, and of interest to readers. The product need not be as original or anticipatory in issue explication as articles in the scholarly journal. It must be pertinent and reflect the prior experience of the readers.

Of all the journal types, the professional journal is the most dependent on the editor for providing almost complete direction. The research and scholarly journal editors work within parameters provided either by their disciplines or by communities of interest. The association journal considers the priorities of the educational association. The professional journal, mailed to readers as a condition of organizational membership, cannot guage its impact or reader interest as measured by subscriptions.

If the research journal editor often feels no need to have a philosophy of education, since it is implied in the role performance, the professional journal leadership frequently enunciates one through contemporary educational aphorisms and points of view. Both types of journals may lack depth; one is intentional and the other is not. Professional journals are likely to have a large number of readers, some of whom communicate with the editor through letters, some of which are published. These journals appear to be very much part of the life of the field.

The Association Journal

Education organizations publish research, scholarly, and professional journals. They also publish association journals that carry organizational news and commentary in columns written by their executives and staff and in articles developed by their editors, in-house authors, and field-based practitioners. Association journals support association directions.

Of the journal types, association journals are least committed to the development of education as a field of study. Of higher priority than for any other publication is its interest in serving both the reader and the publisher, whose positions they perceive as coincident. These journals exist in the political arena and lobby indirectly through official postures shaped as issue-oriented manuscripts, which they disseminate to their regular readers and to individuals in the larger community. This journal type is distinguished from the others by its commitment to influence persons not directly involved in the business of education. It attempts to create linkages with political and other social institutions whose support is necessary for the prosecution of association goals. It is of interest that the most political of the educational journals is also the most expansive in its marketing interests; the most cosmopolitan—the research journal—is the narrowest.

Association journals pursue their goals not only through implicit and explicit advocacy of ideas but also through their support of professional practices that embody the directions deemed important by their publishers. Manuscripts are developed that discuss innovations responsive to associations' priorities. In fact, editors often are required to cajole practitioners to take time away from "work" to share experiences. These rough papers are then rewritten, often shortened, "without violence," and published. In sum, issues and innovations are advocated. It is the editor's responsibility to structure ideas for a field perceived to be planned, hierarchical, and political.

Like their counterparts at professional journals, editors of association journals have multiple job responsibilities. They may edit newsletters, disseminate news releases, and plan conferences. Unlike their counterparts, they may well have journalistic experience and, with it, greater skill at using news and editorial models.

Editorial board members who assist the editor rank high on two dimensions: their abilities to represent reader interests and to work within the framework of objectives established for the journal. These joint commitments reflect the assumed reader-association congruity of purpose. Board members' scholarly and demographic characteristics have very low importance.

If professional journal editors commission manuscripts, the association journal leadership creates them. They have low regard for those scholars who do not communicate well or reflect the critical issues, and they seem to devote as much of their attention to enhancing communication as to the selection of areas that require it. With the research journal editor, the association journal editor places an emphasis on style, but it is the style of everyday communication. Of all the journals, association journals are the clearest in their presentation of values and positions.

WHAT TYPE IS IT?

Although most journals remain in the same mold volume year after volume year, they can and do change. With the appointment of a new editor or the deliberate decision of a publisher, a professional journal can develop into a scholarly publication or vice versa. The notions of "upgrading" or "being responsive to practitioners" may signal such alterations; but they are, in fact, redefinitions of the journal in more fundamental terms. Who becomes the editor or board member, their roles, what is considered knowledge, and how and for what purposes journals are read define type.

These types have been presented here as discrete categories. Journals in transition may be difficult to place. Also, some journals regularly combine elements of different types. A professional journal may have a research department. A research journal published by an association may have a regular column on association-defined issues. Nevertheless, a journal's basic thrust is usually apparent.

The most appropriate directive for the author is to be aware of the motives for his or her work and thus it relevance for a particular type of journal. Not all specialties offer a range of types; of course, many cannot. However, the field does have sufficient resources to allow its members an opportunity to communicate in appropriate ways to colleagues with scholarly or applied interests.

Authors might broaden their range either by communicating with specialists in other areas or by writing to professionals within the broader field. For example, a special educator who typically publishes studies in research journals for other special educators might communicate with specialists in curriculum design or administration through scholarly journals treating curriculum redesign or modification of space for handicapped students. A special educator could also write papers for teachers or school board members who through their professional literature can learn how to implement the intent of new legislation regarding the handicapped.

Authors, over time, create different publishing configurations for themselves. Some only develop manuscripts with one motive; others modify their work during their careers, perhaps by moving from research to professional journals; and still others maintain a diversity both as to type of paper and its readership. There are no value judgements intended here, except that educators ought to exercise conscious choice regarding the development of the direction of their work. Many are socialized into a pattern and believe that that way is the only or best approach. As in other areas, commitments and skills grow, fall into disuse, and are in various stages of development. Educators, during their careers, ought to be able to develop manuscripts that reflect various interests, abilities, and writing goals. This challenge can be met by taking research and writing courses, by maintaining an awareness of the literature in its diversity, and by recognizing the value of the variety of journals that serve our social institution.

Part II
THE MANUSCRIPT
SUBMISSION PROCESS

In Part I, I attempted to demonstrate that the manuscript submission process begins long before a paper is taken to the post office. Manuscripts developed with certain publishing goals make themselves eligible for some journals and ineligible for others.

The chapters in this section have a greater operational orientation. They will assist readers in the process of selecting a journal and understanding its reaction. It is a *process*—eminently rational—that can be executed well, to the benefit of not only one's publishing record but also one's professional satisfaction. Through manuscript submission we can learn a great deal about ourselves and our work.

The chapters in this part deal with pre-submission concerns and actual submission, concentrating on what to expect from editors, reviewers, and copy editors. Last, we will discuss the reasons that manuscripts are accepted and rejected in the journal types presented in Chapter 2.

Chapter 3
PRE-SUBMISSION CONCERNS

PEER REVIEW BEFORE SUBMISSION

At least one colleague, not necessarily at the author's institution, should review a draft of the manuscript and provide as challenging a reaction as possible. Authors are often lax critics of their own work and can easily overlook, misinterpret, or leave unclear an area that if corrected would allow for more favorable editorial response. The development of a support network among colleagues can be among the most important of professional challenges for authors at all stages of their careers. Colleagues provide reactions that not only allow one to improve work but also to defend its value should that be required, and to reaffirm self-confidence should the manuscript be too firmly criticized during the review process. In fact, one of the benefits of presenting a preliminary version of a paper at a conference is the feedback received from peers. If provided first by referees and editors, it is likely to be critical—and final.

Authors should also be aware of the benefits of technical editing. Although consultants are often called upon to provide assistance in the methodological development and execution of work, authors seldom are aware of the availability of talented, professional copy editors, who contribute to the work from a different perspective. The copy editor examines a manuscript not to critique its content or substantive dimensions but to eradicate its writing faults and to improve its flow. Stylistic or grammatical mistakes are frequently systemic: certain words are always used incorrectly, tenses do not agree, pet phrases are used repeatedly, the passive voice detracts. Correcting errors in one paper often prevents their recurrence in others. Challenge and support are available from copy editors as well as from colleagues. These professional consultants are a wise investment, and they can be located in or through university presses, textbook or magazine publishers, and English departments.

ONE FROM THE MANY

After the manuscript has been improved through substantive and editorial consultation and is ready to be typed in final form, the author selects the journal that is most likely to be interested in the topic as treated. What factors should the author take into account?

Author Affiliations

When, how, and why something is written may be an outgrowth of the author's professional and personal interests, commitments, and roles. Authors sustain existing affiliations or develop new ones through their publishing initiatives. They are likely to turn to their professional and scholarly societies, whose publications are distributed to members and which sponsor national meetings at which early forms of the manuscript can be read.

Institutions are placing more and more emphasis on external peer evaluations for judgments as to the worth of a candidate seeking advancement. But at the same time, only a very small percentage of a candidate's colleagues are likely to have read a particular article. An author might consider publishing in a journal whose readers can testify as to the value of the work, individuals who can provide references for promotion or movement to a new setting.

Of course, there are other, possibly more compelling, reasons for publishing in society journals. With readers who can influence the direction of a professional organization, the impact of a timely and persuasive article can alter, however slightly, the orientation of the organization. It might be moved in orientation to a posture more compatible with one's ideas or methods. Also, at the society's meetings, one can pursue the implications of one's ideas or work with individuals interested in replicating or advancing them further.

In all cases, publishing provides opportunities to develop new networks. Many authors make contributions to associations of which they are not members—and in which they do not wish to invest energy—for the rewards of new challenges generated among newly identified colleagues.

As readers, we are aware of colleagues who publish broadly and who are comfortable with a variety of reading communities and others who, though well published, are narrow in their audience focus. Some are highly specialized in their work for member readerships who are unable to critique the quality of work but who can marvel at the cognitive gymnastics of a colleague; others communicate to more professionally "appreciative" readerships. After all, most writers belong to more than one professional organization, and each does have very different qualities from the others.

In some senses we define who we are by what we publish, for whom, and for responses that we can predict, at least on the broad level. We create our own critiques, or not, as well as opportunities, through what we publish. The considerations we use to choose our audiences raise value and ethical issues that authors should address.

Journal Characteristics

In the previous chapter we examined the ways in which journals differ in their basic orientations; they also have distinct operational and procedural characteristics that should be considered when choosing one for manuscript submission.

The first is the frequency of publication. Journals publish monthly, quarterly, and biannually. As a rule, the more frequent the appearance, the earlier one's paper is likely to be published. In spite of the delays about which authors complain, which are caused, it should be noted, by printing schedules as well as by manuscript backlogs, many journals have on file articles for but one or two issues at any time. It is indeed a myth that editors are overwhelmed by quality manuscripts that must take their turns at the end of a long line. The line for most journals is not very long, and thus the frequency of publication is some indicator of turnover. A few journals publish in each issue a list of titles of manuscripts that have been accepted and await publication. An author can estimate "in press" time by comparing previous issues' lists and actual publication dates. Also, some education publications indicate in the published article the date the initial manuscript or revision was received.

A very important consideration related to frequency is a journal's mix of uninvited papers and invited papers or commissioned special issues. For example, a quarterly journal may set aside but one issue per volume for unsolicited manuscripts. The issue might consist of the three best manuscripts out of 200 received. In fact, this quarterly is a small annual with low acceptance odds.

In addition to frequency, authors should be aware of circulation figures as indicators of the number of readers, though the two are hardly the same. A list of 5,000 paying subscribers might reflect a more active, committed readership than 15,000 recipients of a journal distributed as part of association membership benefits. Some journals have a strong library circulation and student readers but few individual subscribers. Others, more recently founded, may have few of either.

Circulation figures are available in an issue published near the end or beginning of the calendar year when journals are required to publish a statement of ownership, management, and circulation to comply with second-class mailing requirements. Figures are also available in a number of reference works intended for both authors and advertisers.

A third characteristic is a journal's orientation to state, regional, national, or even international readerships. It should not be assumed that a geographically delimited readership is less desirable. The author must make a judgment regarding the scope of a paper as defined by geographic boundaries. A comparative study, for example, may be appropriate for an international publication, but it may also have a regional interest if the issues treated are especially pertinent to the region.

Authors ought to consider journals' reputations for dependability in reviewing manuscripts in a timely fashion. Although editors may inform authors that the review period will take eight to twelve weeks and referees are expected to observe such a schedule when they assume review assignments, inordinate delays are the pattern for some publications. Formal guides, which appear in Appendix A, supply some data regarding the review period, but the most valid information is likely to be obtained from colleagues whose work has appeared in a journal or from those whose work has been rejected but who are willing to discuss the review process. All journals are subject to occasional inordinate delays because of uncooperative referees. For a particular author the costs of such delay may be too high, regardless of the pattern.

Speed of publication is less an issue in the sciences where authors typically have grant funds to pay for page charges; journals add pages if authors purchase them. Few social science publications charge authors printing fees; many do, however, charge submission fees to cover processing expenses. Except for the occasional professional journal in education that pays authors for commissioned papers, authors and journals do not exchange funds in our field. (The apparent exceptions to this rule are unrelated to editorial decisions: an author is usually required to pay for drafting artwork for any illustrations not supplied with the accepted manuscript, for excessive alterations in galley proofs, and for reprints of the article.)

Although journals do not charge authors for disseminating articles in the interests of the field and professional organizations do not require one to be a member in order to submit a manuscript, authors must not assume that journals are on sound economic footing. Many are in precarious financial situations, supported by professional societies and universities that are themselves facing uncertain futures. Editors and referees contribute much of their time "for the good of the field" and expect authors to match their commitment by subscribing to the publications through which they receive their rewards. Editors often wonder why they should be more accountable to authors than authors are to the publishers that promote their ideas.

Fifth, journals are property, and their gatekeepers exercise property rights. Editors and editorial boards who manage them represent various backgrounds, which authors should consider in relation to their manuscripts. Given the gatekeepers' schooling and approaches to scholarship, is it likely that there will be *basic* acceptance of the methods employed in a particular manuscript? Authors would do well to assume that editors and referees wear blinders, that they have biases that often operate even if they are not recognized. It is not unusual for referees to understand poorly, misinterpret, or find inappropriate legitimate approaches to knowledge creation that are foreign to them. Authors then would wisely learn about the gatekeepers and at least attempt to educate them through footnotes or appendices should it appear likely that a work will not have an equal opportunity.

The topical and methodological interests of the gatekeepers are not the only ones the author should consider: there are ideological and mechanical ones as well. A manuscript will appear in company with others' work, and the placement should be comfortable. Does the editor place prestige names as the lead articles and place the less visible toward the rear? Are papers not in sympathy with the vested interests of an association used, implicity or explicity, as vehicles for critical reactions by others who have truth on their side? Do papers seem to be published in order of acceptance? Are they grouped by topic area, suggesting that an article might be delayed until a mass of papers on the same theme is available? How do the papers read? Does it appear that authors' personalities are evident, or are the articles very much alike? Homogeneity may be the result of the selection process or a very active copy editor who practically rewrites the accepted work. No author expects violence to be done to his or her ideas or manner of expression, yet this often occurs.

The last characteristic that authors should consider is the journal as a physical product. Is the journal carefully produced? Are there numerous typos and incorrect references? Is the binding likely to crack after a few uses? Is the type size large enough to be easily legible? Are the margins sufficient for readers' annotations? Are articles squeezed out by advertisements? Is the current issue current? It is certainly desirable to be published in carefully produced, well-designed, long-lasting journals that demand to be read and used.

In summary, authors should weigh such journal characteristics as frequency of publication, circulation, geographic orientation, timely treatment of manuscripts, charges, gatekeeper characteristics, foci of other authors, copy editor initiatives, and physical qualities.

Journal Interests

Authors should attempt to develop an intimate familiarity with what the journal "says," implicitly, regarding its topical interests.

Some editors preface each issue with a review of contents, using adjectives and adverbs that suggest why papers were accepted. Editors also write columns in which they discuss the qualities and characteristics they seek in manuscripts and the topics authors might address. A good way to discover editorial interests is to examine the final issues under one editor's leadership and the first or second number under a new editor. A journal's history, intentions, and premises are usually noted at those times. Even without these comments, many journals publish, or make available for the asking, instructions to contributors that go beyond aphoristic expectations. These directions can provide expert guidance.

Authors should also study old and recent issues. Journals not only address the future through what they publish, but they also maintain continuity with their pasts. Journals have traditions, and editors maintain them. It is striking how some editorial statements written decades ago when the education environment was very different retain an adequate contemporary value.

Careful attention should obtain on an operational as well as a strategic level. For example, a journal's title is important; in fact, if authors paid more attention to them, one of the major causes of rejection would be eliminated. As cases in point, a higher education journal will not consider manuscripts on teacher education even though it occurs in a university; an education finance journal will not consider a manuscript on instructional technology, even if it is cost-effective.

Further, authors should examine carefully the last two volume years of journals being considered. Except in the case of journals that advance existing knowledge, editors play a significant role in creating the mixture of papers that are published. What will be published is often what has been published, with predictable modifications. For example, if a journal publishes a paper on the value of marketing in college admissions, it is likely to accept a later one on marketing strategies and techniques, and a subsequent one on the pitfalls of strategies based on current experiences. However, this journal might never again publish a paper on the need to use marketing in college admissions—unless a new editor unfamiliar with what the journal has published were to begin the series again. Editors attempt to maintain continuity, and authors who are aware of the patterns, their gaps and possible extensions, have better opportunities at particular times for specific publications. As in any relationship, the author-editor relationship is likely to be more successful if joint or complementary needs are met.

The final suggested method for learning about publications'

interests, short of writing to inquire—which we will address below—is by attending meetings of associations' publications committees or reading their minutes in organizational newsletters. Not only can authors meet editors to discuss manuscript ideas, they can also learn about opportunities to serve as referees and book reviewers. More than one editor learned about editorial openings through such meetings.

ADDITIONAL SUGGESTIONS

At this point we will assume that the author has considered all of the factors and has chosen the journal that would seem to be interested in the form of scholarship, the topic, and the direction a manuscript takes.

Inquiry to the Editor

Authors intimately familiar with the journal to which they intend to submit their work need not write or call editors in order to assess interest. Should an author attempt such contacts, the effort is likely to be greeted with a variety of reactions depending on the journal type. Research journal editors may resent such queries, for they expect authors to recognize that methodological parameters, implicitly, drive papers and that they cannot be assessed through a sketchy statement. Scholarly journal editors are more likely to respond, possibly in form letters by indicating that the topic or treatment seems within or outside the journal's focus. Both professional and association journal editors, taking a more active role in the creation of published work, are likely to provide greater direction based on their priorities.

As a general rule for all types, but especially for the first two, it is inappropriate to ask the editor for pre-submission guidance on the development of an unsolicited manuscript. The editor is not the author and has no interest in being co-opted; neither should it be assumed that the editor has time to shape the submission.

Multiple Submissions

Although the manuscript review period can be lengthy, turning a timely manuscript into a dated one, an author is not justified in submitting a paper simultaneously to more than one journal. The injunction against multiple submissions is a cardinal rule in publishing. Editors and referees contribute a great deal of uncompen-

sated time for the review of colleagues' work. Trusting to professional rather than entreprenurial norms, they expect to have
access to a manuscript until or unless it is returned to the author.
Those seeking to have a work published in more than one journal
at a time have engaged in a variety of unethical and even illegal
practices. Such practices, if discovered, can result in harsh letters
from the editors of the aggrieved publications, but even more
important, if such occurrences are repeated, they may very well
result in informal blacklisting.

Transmittal of the Manuscript

The final version of the manuscript should be prepared in accordance with the typing and stylistic instructions that appear in
the journal's guidelines to contributors. Guidelines are typically
published in the journal; if not, they can be obtained from the
editorial office. Authors should also examine current articles as
stylistic models.

Editors take different positions regarding the consideration of
manuscripts prepared in non-house style. Some believe it is inappropriate to demand that authors, with limited resources, retype
papers for each submission; an accepted manuscript can be prepared in appropriate form during the typically requested revision
stage. Other editors believe that papers should be immediately
publishable if accepted and will return unreviewed those manuscripts that are not in the house style.

Obviously, it is safer to follow the second assumption; it is also
politically wiser. As we will discuss later, editor's initial reactions
to manuscripts are the most critical. Following house style helps
shape positive editorial expectations, in part by suggesting that
the work was written especially for the editor's journal.

Clean, accurate copies are a must. They should be carefully
proofed, not only by the typist and author but by one or two
others who might notice easily overlooked errors. Incorrect
spelling, especially of names, and even minor typographical errors
reduce the credibility of a manuscript; such slips cannot be afford-
ed. Presentation is also enhanced through use of carbon rather
than conventional ribbon and good quality bond and copy paper
stock. Do not send yellowed, repeatedly stapled copies suggesting
a long line of rejections. Although "image management" may be

too strong a term to describe typescript preparation, clean, elegant, easily read manuscripts, assist editors who make rapid assessments; as an author you want to hold editors' attention. Substantive merit is, of course, the most important factor, but the care exercised by the author in meeting journal style and presenting material clearly are noticed, even if only on an unconscious level.

For research and scholarly journals, editors instruct authors to remove self-reference from the manuscripts so that referees will not be swayed by personal or demographic factors. Authors should remove self-reference throughout, not only on the cover page, but in footnotes, references, and acknowledgments, and should not reproduce copies on institutionally water-marked bond. It is appropriate to send, properly labelled, an untouched original and copies on which demographic material has been excised for referee circulation.

Manuscripts should be submitted in the required number of copies and, if requested, a stamped self-addressed envelope enclosed. As absurd as it might seem, some authors fail to keep a copy in their files. Although infrequent, papers are lost in transit.

The final action is writing a transmittal letter to accompany the manuscript. The author should, of course, insure that it is addressed to the current editor at the correct address. It is not uncommon for editors to receive material addressed to forebears twice removed, perhaps even long after their death, a situation that makes for an awkward introduction of prospective author to editor.

The author should not enclose a vita or picture, which occurs more frequently than might be expected. The manuscript persuades, and authors who rely on race or experience or doctoral origins to support their ideas are not warmly received. If the author is acquainted with the editor, there is no need to remind the recipient of such familiarity unless the editor specifically requested or recommended a submission through some interaction. The editor feels a need to be free from suggestions of biases, even if they in fact operate. It is also suggested that authors not indicate that promotion or tenure rests on the editorial decision. Editors are all too aware of the possible impact of their actions and do not need to be reminded of the burden.

Editors do not want to be told how relevant the work is to the readership; that is their judgment. They also would rather not hear that all of the author's colleagues have persuaded him or her to submit the work. The author is accountable, and the only peer reactions that count are the referees'. Authors risk the immediate return of a paper if they request an immediate editorial decision. Authors often make such requests in order to rationalize an expected rejection on substantive grounds.

Authors should simply write that they are enclosing a particular manuscript, possibly reiterate the abstract, and thank the editor for attending to it. They can record their expectation to hear from the editor within a reasonable time, say, three months. (Of course, the author is free to inquire about the publishing decision should the reaction not be made in the period specified.)

Many journals routinely acknowledge the receipt of a manuscript, but the inclusion of a self-addressed postcard is proper and guarantees notice of the paper's arrival. Most editors can recall letters from authors six months after the mailing of a manuscript asking about its disposition, only to learn it never arrived.

The manuscript, copies, and transmittal letter should be securely packaged and affixed with adequate first-class postage. Before sealing, authors should once again inspect the manuscripts for page sequencing and to assure that all tables, appendices, notes, and citation lists are in place. Some journals request a postage-paid, self-addressed envelope for the return of the manuscript should it fail to be accepted. The original should be retrieved for possible resubmission; the copies will be redone, but since referees frequently make marginal comments, the author may wish to receive them as well.

Now the anxiety begins.

Chapter 4
SUBMITTING THE MANUSCRIPT: WHAT TO EXPECT

In this chapter we move below the global and strategic level and examine more specific elements of the author-publication relationship. Of course, even with a more focused approach, we will be discussing behaviors in general terms. Obviously, on one level, each journal's history and current practice shape actions that are, for it, normative; and various authors submitting manuscripts to the same publication are likely to have different tales to tell because of undiscussed assumptions and hidden presuppositions. With this in mind, we are able to proceed in our discussion of journal responsiveness.

THE NEED FOR INTIMATE FAMILIARITY

In addition to leading to better manuscript placements, intimate familiarity with specific publications helps compensate for the poor communication that many journals have with prospective authors. In a study I conducted to investigate the behavior of education editors (Silverman, 1976a) I discovered that fewer than half of the field's journals publish a statement of their broad objectives or discuss their policies relevant to the evaluation of manuscripts. In fact, even upon the rejection of a manuscript, 30 percent of the journals use a form letter to communicate with authors.

As is true for many systems, journals often protect themselves by failing to announce their procedures and cloaking behaviors in rhetoric designed to forestall further inquiry. Accountability, with its ethical dimensions, is a rightful concern of authors, if not of this book, and can be demonstrated through assertive expressions of interest to publishers and editorial boards. It is healthy if chagrin is not accompanied with surprise when authors detect "mystery-mastery" behavior.

Recognizing, then, that it is the author's responsibility to understand the maze for specific journals, what should the author expect after a paper is submitted?

THE EDITOR'S ACTIONS: RECEIPT AND INITIAL TREATMENT
The First Step

The manuscript arrives at the editorial office.* Upon receipt, a secretary or assistant editor logs in the manuscript and may assign it a number that all parties then use in referring to the paper. The editor examines it, with or without the transmittal letter. Some editors do not want to know the author's identity or affiliation; most do. It is common for manuscripts to be refereed "blindly" by outside readers; the in-house reviews are commonly made with an awareness of authors' demographic characteristics.

Although such personalistic knowledge may result in bias, the intent is quite different. Many editors require author data in order to make valid referee assignments. It is commonly accepted that manuscripts should not be reviewed by persons who are or have been associated directly or indirectly with the author. Thus, a person who was a former advisee or advisor or had a common advisor or had sustained contact through employment is, in most cases, ruled out as a referee.

Although it is often charged that authors from less well known institutions and women and minorities, regardless of location, are penalized by editor biases, the reverse may also be true. Many editors feel special responsibilities to different author classes. For example, more careful attention, more extensive feedback, and greater encouragement are frequently given to "new" authors who might be severely disillusioned by initial rejection. A negative or positive bias is unlikely to exist for women, minorities, or less prestigiously connected authors; on the other hand, editors are biased regarding the well known and more advantaged in that they expect more from them. An author giving less than one would expect to be his or her best is likely to affront an editor. Although insulted, some editors will publish mediocre or worse material from the well known; many will not.

It might be appropriate for editors to read the transmittal letter and other author-identifying material after reaching a decision on

*Individuals personally acquainted with the editor may mail papers directly to professorial offices or home addresses, a practice not advocated as it assumes the editor will make a friendly decision. Of course, the paper is more likely to be lost or misplaced.

whether to return the paper to the author or to send it to a referee. Such a procedure is not common. From the very beginning, for most journals, a response is being shaped; and extrinsic as well as intrinsic data affect the response. Thus, the manuscript and transmittal letter are brought to the editor's attention in order for the initial set of decisions to be made.

The editor's first concern is whether the paper is "appropriate" to the journal and its readership. The editor skims the manuscript to discover its salient meaning; to assess whether the readership, within broad parameters, is likely to have both an interest in the topic and a background in the methodology or practice to the degree that the paper will reflect the state of the art as the audience understands it; to determine, by examining the references, if the manuscript is dated; to search for critical flaws, such as miscitations or misspellings of cited authors' names, to learn not if the author has been careful but if he or she has not been careful; to learn if the paper has been presented in accordance with the journal's stylistic guidelines and if the manuscript has been composed with at least an acceptable minimum of skill; to consider it in the context of other recently published papers and those under revision and in press; to learn how congruent the paper is with current editorial or associational commitments; to determine if the author has written previously on the same subject and whether the data or positions in the manuscript are in fact new; to examine manuscript length; to make a prognosis as to how much editorial work a paper may need or to estimate typesetting requirements, as illustrations, tables, and mathematics may be more expensive to set than straight text; and to ascertain how difficult it will be to identify referees, should the topic be atypical or the author's work known to the majority of those knowledgeable in an area.

In addition to these considerations are the more personalistic ones referred to earlier: the previous or current relationship with the author; the author's sex, institutional location, and vested interests that may be similar to the editor's demographic characteristics. These factors influence editor's judgments in individual ways.

All of these factors, in different combinations and with various strengths, inform the editor's decision either to return a manuscript to the author at this point or to proceed with further review.

If the paper is returned, the editor may or may not take pains to respond personally to the author. An editor might send a form letter indicating how overburdened with good papers the journal is, or a letter may have a checklist of possible problems with marks made in the appropriate boxes. Editors may respond in greater or lesser detail, more or less substantively, and with or without suggestions as to other journals that might have an interest in the paper, or with recommendations for revisions the author might make to enhance the probability of acceptance in the journal of submission or other publications. Of course, for this last item, the opposite is also true: recommendations are not made to chill the possibility of resubmission.

A great deal, then, depends on many explicit and implicit assumptions, minor judgments, and the ethical and value positions of the editor.

In a minority of journals an in-house staff receives and comments on a manuscript before it reaches the editor, who will then decide its fate. Editors who use this method indicate that their staff members, through a good deal of experience and familiarity with the agency's needs, can spot a potentially usable paper. Obviously, formal credentials or position often have little to do with competency, and a well-chosen staff can make excellent recommendations. Regardless, some gatekeepers' decisions are heavily influenced by early in-house opinion.

The Second Step

Manuscripts that pass the initial reading are sent to persons whose reactions can assist the editor in making a good decision regarding acceptability.

Under the assumption that pooled judgments are more valid than a single judgment, research and scholarly journals usually request readings from at least two referees. Three readers may be required if there is basic disagreement between the initial two or if a narrow expertise on some element of a manuscript is necessary. The readers are peer experts in areas treated in the manuscript.

Reviews are no less important for professional or association journals, but they need not be accomplished by a specific number of readers. These journals may request one external reading or a single in-house review. In fact, if there are multiple internal readings, it is likely that hierarchical as well as expert values will be evident: supervisory judgments will be made implicitly on subordinates' reactions to the manuscript.

There are additional elements that impinge on the number of referees used for judgments on a manuscript: the expertise of the editor and the editor's "ownership" of the journal. Editors are often well grounded in the dimensions that might be presented in a manuscript. But self-appraised "expertise" often expands in parallel with one's ego. Although there are few Renaissance men, there are broadly educated generalists; there are also persons who mistakenly regard "awareness" as "understanding." The larger the editor's self-conception, the smaller the number of referees used.

Some editors have goals they wish to attain during short terms of office and perceive themselves as trustees of the field. Other editors believe their journals are theirs, to represent their points of view, whether in the form of questions needing attention, methodologies meriting visibility, or issues and opinions requiring airing. A high degree of editor ownership, like expertise, results not only in fewer requested referee judgments but also in predispositions on how those reactions are used.

The editor's choice of referees will be influenced by attitudes related to self-definition as well as journal type. According to type, editors are likely to perceive themselves as promoters of significant science, stimulators of scholarship having catalytic value, supporters of fresh ideas, or spokespersons for certain interests. The referees who are selected will reflect both the more formal and the less explicit role definitions, organizational relationships, and, as noted, values and assumptions. Given the variety of choices that could result from these combinations, it is not possible to delineate all of the possible relationships, but the following are a sample.

Editors may use experts, whether their focus is substance, method, or practice, but some will have broader and others narrower world views. Some will balance their critiques and give the author the benefit of the doubt. Some will attempt to impress and coopt the editor and dazzle or put down the author. The editor knows very soon who these people are and uses them deliberately. At times an editor will mix and match: one substantive expert and one generalist. At times a curious parochialism is evident: substantive experts will be used, but they will be from the editor's home university. This suggests the intrusion of power and exchange relationships of a sort different from what might be expected. Reviewers may be used because they are known to accept or reject most of what they receive.

The commonly held conception is that objectivity reigns. This is probably accurate, on one level. However, there are hidden dimensions about which most authors are unaware and most editors uninterested in exploring. These second-order concerns do not bring the procedures into question as much as the norms and values that guide behavior.

The Third Step

A standardized form upon which referees are to record their critiques is usually sent with the manuscript. The editor establishes categories that others will react to and upon which the manuscript will be judged and the decision on publication based. Some review sheets enumerate many form and content items, for example, the length of the manuscript and its originality, and call for grades from A to D; contain sections for direct responses addressed to the author and to the editor; and include space for a recommendation regarding acceptability. Some editors do not specify more than a few items for referee comment and expect a more open reaction; others might through their instructions specify a variety of approaches to inquiry (or elements within a number of approaches), such as action research or theory building, so that the referees will read the paper with similar assumptions. In brief, the editor provides the vehicle, through the review sheet, upon which the manuscript is viewed.

The review sheet also establishes referee expectations of other sorts—the amount of open space allows for just so much feedback to the author, a separate section addressed confidentially to the editor prompts the airing of affective reactions and instructions, a recommendation to publish early or late influences the appearance of other work and the reward system based on publication.

Authors should expect the review sheets to reflect validly the field or practice area and to promote the quality of reactions that will lead to meaningful advice to them and quality papers for the journal. Too tight, they rid the referee of unique and well-considered reactions; too loose, they fail to reflect the editor's and author's needs; too narrow, they exclude the alternatives upon which an emerging field is based; too catholic, they suggest that everything is of equal value; too terse, they obscure the meaning of such terms as "originality" or "appropriate" to which referees respond; too lengthy in enumeration of items, they imply that the acceptable manuscript should be mechanical. Authors should have an intense interest in the template placed over their work.

Referees at times write their criticisms directly on the manuscript, although very useful to authors. This practice does not allow the paper to be mailed elsewhere. As noted above, editors over time learn who are the hard graders, how they differ in their expectations, who they believe the average or optimal reader is, how much assistance they expect the editor to need and in what areas, even how threatened they are by work not their own, and how celebratory. Authors should expect that such familiarity will result in the selection of referees whose approach is compatible with the editor's leadership.

The Fourth Step

The referee returns the completed review sheets, along with the manuscript, to the editor—preferably after a reasonably short period of time. The editor, at this point, usually examines the referee's work more for adequacy of treatment and possible bias, often evidenced by excesses of praise or blame, than for direct editorial advice. The editor must decide whether to continue the refereeing process by asking additional reviewers to comment on specific points called into question in the initial review.

Regardless of the editor's opinion on the merits of a negative review, in certain cases the reviewer's negativity may corroborate the editor's impression of the paper and suggest that it does not deserve the expenditure of additional review resources. That is, a negative review may not be on the mark but close enough that the editor can use it to reach or justify a decision on rejection.

On the other hand, negative reviews may prompt the editor to seek additional judgments if it is clear that the creativity or originality reflected in the manuscript was not understood or appreciated by the inital reviewers. Such decisions are influenced by the editor's strengths and biases as educator—as well as by whether there is a backlog of manuscripts.

The Fifth Step

If the overall quality of the referees' reports is satisfactory, the editor studies them carefully along with the manuscript. The editor typically rejects or accepts the manuscript following this examination, or notes major or minor flaws in the work, which, if corrected, would result in acceptance.

The editor, not the referees, makes the final decision; the judgments and recommendations of referees are key determinants in the decision, but editors and referees may not be in agreement. For example, a referee may recommend rejection on, say, stylistic grounds, while the editor finds that the paper's overall strengths qualify it for acceptance. Referees may cause a paper to become dated by drawing out the review process inordinately, with the result that the editor may accept, for reasons of equity, a paper that is deemed dated.

The editor's response to the author at this point can be brief or expansive and detailed. The editor can convey the referees' reactions in whole or in part. Usually the referees' comments are edited, with the deletion of any ad hominem or other derogatory remarks, such as unflattering comparisons between the referee's own powerful work and the work under review. On the other hand, the editor may delete from the reviews those judgements that do not support the editor's decision; thus the author might not learn of suggestions for changes that the editor feels are unnecessary; positive findings that apparently do not accord with the decision against acceptance; or management-related remarks, such as a referee's promise that a manuscript would be accepted if certain changes were to be made.

If the manuscript is not rejected, the editor indicates to the author what revisions are required to put it in acceptable form. Such recommendations take the form of conditional acceptance or outright acceptance with the understanding that the author will perform the recommended revisions. The paper that is submitted ready for publication is rare. How the editor approaches the author with regard to revision is based not only on the number and severity of problems in the paper but also on the editor's level of interest in it—Will an author choose to send the paper elsewhere rather than revise it?—and the length of the backlog of unpublished manuscripts.

Editors may use the continuum "reject/major—minor revision/ accept" but are more likely to be more complex. A request for a major revision might be accompanied with strong support statements, or none; with an outline of approaches to handling the problem, or none. A request for minor revision might emphasize that the changes are easily accomplished; or it might be "cut and dried," suggesting the journal cares neither about the paper nor its author.

In brief, the editor might act as an educator or a guard, as an interpreter or a transmitter, as a colleague or a bureaucrat, depending on personal definitions discussed earlier, the perceived value of a paper, and the characteristics and behavior of the author. Although editors' reactions, in general, are based on a variety of interacting factors, each editor tends to follow an individual underlying pattern. Authors are unlikely to be able to grasp these patterns, but publication committees and agencies can discover them by evaluating editor behavior, by creating conditions for dialogue between writers and editors, and by developing appeal procedures for authors. Authors should expect editors to discuss periodically their procedures, both in editorial statements and during conference programs; they should also expect a prompt, caring treatment of their manuscript.

On the other hand, authors should be aware of the multiple demands on the editor and reviewer, who frequently find themselves deluged by manuscripts. Further, it is sometimes difficult to find reviewers for some work. But, most importantly, authors should be aware that reviewers approach with less enthusiasm, and react more slowly to, pedestrian papers than to those that assist them in expanding their understanding. Delays are caused as much by shallow work as by the multiple responsibilities of editors and referees.

Good editing, like good teaching and good administering, is more than the result of certain strategic and tactical behaviors. It is an attitude; and for some, even more: it is a way of life.

THE REVIEWER'S ACTIONS

Referees, whether internal or external, have three audiences: field or agency, the editor, and the author. The reviewer's definitions of these audiences, preceding and during the examination, provide the frameworks for content-oriented reactions.

Reviewers are selected because they have expertise or eminence, or both, in a field or agency. Depending on the journal type, readers are concerned that a paper make a contribution to the larger system. Obviously, such a criterion glosses over certain critical dimensions about which editors may be less than clear, to themselves and to the referees.

What constitutes a contribution? What should be a paper's impact? Should a manuscript be developed for the field broadly or for a narrower readership? How large is the system? Does it include other disciplines or social institutions? What are the publishing priorities? How many are there and in what order? What should be the relations between what a paper demonstrates and how it is demonstrated?

The answers to these and similar questions are implied in referees' reactions to the conventional items of interest to editors. We may not want or expect our referees to be educational philosophers, but it might be appropriate if they could clarify their positions on such questions to enable the field to understand the meaning of abbreviated reactions, written in haste. What does a high or low grade for originality, validity of thought, topical value, and interest to readers mean?

The review is written primarily for the editor, who will use the advice and recommendations to make a decision. But what are the characteristics of the reviewer, and how is the editor-reviewer relationship perceived? There may be differences, of course, in formal status and informal reputation that have implications too numerous to mention and, at time, too subtle to diagnose well. For example, how is an education full professor, as editor, at a minor university perceived by a sociologist assistant professor, as referee, at a distinguished university? In what ways will this relationship be defined through the strength or directness or care of a reaction? Experience suggests that younger faculty develop more thorough reviews. They may be close to the current literature, but they also want to impress the editor, to suggest that their own manuscripts will evidence the same critical strengths they demand in others' work. It is one thing for an editor to be aware of such a pattern and another to know what to do about it.

In addition to status differences, the editor will be perceived, in relation to the topic treated in the manuscript, on a continuum between nonexpert and expert, on different cognitive levels. The reviewer may be more or less explicit about his or her assumptions of the editor's knowledge. For example, a reviewer might know that the editor lacks expertise in an area but may not wish to risk insulting the editor by explaining elementary points. This could result in an "as you know" review. Of course, the editor does not know.

Further, the referee places the editor on another continuum, which can be labelled "insider-outsider." This interacts with a similar continuum on which the referee can be located. Many editors are not central figures in their field's work and/or the scholarship area represented by the manuscript. (Silverman, 1976b) Referees may explain or provide background to educate the editor as prelude to the decision. As an example of the latter, the referee may share insider biases they would not own up to publicly. A reviewer might note that certain important individuals reacted negatively to the paper when it was read some months earlier at a conference or that a paper conflicts with the posture of a prestigious agency. The innuendoes are more important than the review as presented.

The referee also perceives the editor as a judge. Just as these officials can be liberal or conservative and assume greater or lesser control in their courts, so it is with the editor. Does the referee believe the editor is looking for reasons to convict or acquit, for balanced and empathic remarks or hostile reactions? Does a critic overstate a case to compete with anticipated strong reactions from other referees? Does the reviewer care about the other witnesses? Does the referee hope to grow by learning others' reactions and, similarly, to assist in the development of other critics? Assuming a variety of implicit negotiations among parties to the review process, does the reviewer believe in bargaining or in problem solving as the most appropriate mode? Clearly, reviewer expectations of the editor as judge are critical.

Of less importance than these factors is the reviewer's expectations of the editor as publisher. It is common for readers to suggest "publish if you have room" or "publish early." The latter assumes the editor's interest in advancing some work at the expense of other accepted material for reasons informed by a "competition" metaphor. These special papers may be touted to increase circula-

tion, attract better manuscripts, and even to be noted in a prestigious newspaper. Although the degree of entreprenurial interest
is influenced by journal type, it would be an error to understate
its relevance to reviewers (and editors) who perceive instrumental
value in it.

The referee, then, is responsive to both the field or agency and
to the editor in terms of answers to self-generated questions,
assumptions, and expectations.

The referee's third client, the author, may be acquainted with
the referee, who will have to deal with the manuscript in relation
to their history. Of course, a number of assumptions can be made
regarding the author on the basis of demographic qualities, regardless of personal familiarity. The referee is unlikely to know the
author's identity if the manuscript is reviewed blind, though frequently specialists can intelligently guess the origin of a paper.

As is true for teachers, referees can be caring, abusive, mature,
adolescent, terse, discursive, generous, stern, mentoring, possessive,
intelligent, or dense. They frequently are inconsistent in their tone
and recommendations to the editor and to the author. Following
a few paragraphs to the author suggesting revisions that might
improve a paper, the referee might write to the editor that it
would appear unlikely that the paper could be improved. Such a
set of reactions raises obvious ethical issues, which cannot be
treated here.

Certainly, many referees are consistent in their remarks to
both the editor and the author. Authors should expect mature,
professional treatment from referees and should also hope that the
ideas in the manuscript are "forgotten" immediately after the review process. Unless and until published, the knowledge does not
exist. It should not inform, in any way, the work of those involved
in the review process. Inasmuch as referees agree to read partly
to keep abreast with new developments, this is an impossible
expectation to maintain. Although editors usually request the return of a manuscript following its examination, photocopying,
note taking, or simple memory cannot be effectively challenged.

This chapter focuses on what authors might expect from editors
and referees. The reader is likely to be both overwhelmed with
the possibilities and less than satisfied with the indirect responses.
Except for "hoping for the best," which clearly is inadequate, the

prime guarantor of acceptable and appropriate behavior is to create and use avenues for dialogue among interested parties. There should be expanded opportunities for persons involved in editing and reviewing to confront the relevant issues, to learn how to perform more adequately, to report to their constituencies, and to solve problems with better prepared publications committees and editorial boards.

We perceive authors as being dependent on the judgments of others and expect that they will learn from their critics. Interdependency and learning must be assumed among all who are involved in the publishing process. Greater accountability will result from the consideration of relevant assumptions, value and behavior patterns; and the premise underlying better accountability might very well read, "Do not do to others that which you would not have them do to you."

Chapter 5
THE CRITERIA EDITORS USE

In earlier sections of this book we addressed the strategic relationships between paper and journal. Manuscripts have a greater opportunity for acceptance if they relate appropriately to the journal's current interests, as demonstrated through its publishing history and its current contents, and if the cognitive socialization of the gatekeepers is taken into account by authors.

Here we examine specific criteria, by journal type, that editors, in response to a survey questionnaire, have deemed more or less important in the selection of manuscripts. The reader is cautioned that an individual editor may use criteria that are not included among those noted below and that patterns of criteria or their relative weights may differ from journal to journal. Although we once again urge readers to be intimately familiar with journals of interest, we suggest that the criteria appearing below may serve usefully as filters for reconstructing and considering the thought patterns of editors and referees.

These criteria are categorized in two groups: process and content. The former describe the norms and values implicit in manuscripts, as well as their organization. The latter are focused on data collection and use and their orientation to the field of education. The reader should be aware that the substantive meaning of the criteria are dependent to some degree on an editor's professional perspectives. For example, although "theory" or "originality" may be similarly defined by all editors, the words have connotations and operational meanings for research journal editors that are at variance with those held by association journal editors. These contextual definitions will be alluded to and are part of the framework constructed in previous chapters.

The Data

In research on the behavior of education journal editors, we requested respondents from the full range of journals to react to the following (Silverman, 1978): "Editors and reviewers of manuscripts base their decisions on the acceptability of manuscripts on a variety of criteria. Please indicate the importance of the following criteria as they relate to your journal." One hundred and thirty editors responded, and their weightings of the relative significance of criteria appear below in Tables I and II.

Table I

PROCESS CRITERIA FOR MANUSCRIPT ACCEPTABILITY*

Criteria	Total x̄	Total S.D.	Research x̄	Research S.D.	Scholarly x̄	Scholarly S.D.	Professional x̄	Professional S.D.	Association x̄	Association S.D.
Clarity and conciseness of writing	4.12	0.81	4.00	0.60	4.35	0.67	3.98	0.72	4.20	1.24
Appropriateness of manuscript's total organization	3.95	1.04	4.16	0.71	4.21	0.78	3.81	1.02	3.76	1.51
Validity of logic used	3.91	0.92	4.16	0.71	4.24	0.83	3.72	1.00	3.66	0.76
Spirited style	3.44	0.96	2.27	0.90	3.48	0.83	3.50	0.96	3.88	0.75
Compatability with disciplinary ethics	3.31	1.08	3.70	0.82	3.54	0.90	3.11	1.24	3.17	1.01
Appropriate use of statistics	3.29	1.22	4.33	0.65	3.51	1.12	2.90	1.22	3.29	1.26
Suggestions for future research/thought/action	3.22	1.11	3.27	0.78	3.29	1.17	3.24	1.14	2.94	1.08
Theoretically grounded	3.14	1.10	3.75	0.75	3.44	1.08	2.96	1.08	2.64	1.16
Discussion of limitations of data or theory	2.87	0.95	3.25	0.96	3.08	0.98	2.72	0.82	2.58	1.12
Development of alternative interpretation of data presented	2.73	0.85	3.00	0.63	2.91	0.84	2.60	0.82	2.58	1.06
Review of literature	2.66	1.15	3.36	0.80	3.02	1.11	2.42	1.07	2.17	1.28
Replicability (if research article)	2.56	1.25	3.54	0.68	2.69	1.34	2.45	1.20	1.86	1.06
Emotional neutrality of the author	2.54	1.06	3.54	0.93	2.62	1.06	2.44	0.93	2.05	1.14
Reputation of the author or institution	2.51	1.30	1.41	0.66	2.27	1.30	2.75	1.29	3.05	1.14
Use of standard empirical methodologies	2.45	1.04	3.40	0.69	2.71	1.15	2.16	0.89	2.17	0.95
Adherence to journal's stylistic guidelines	2.44	1.12	3.09	1.04	2.43	1.14	2.28	1.05	2.52	1.28
Use of experimental as opposed to non-experimental designs	2.42	1.05	3.18	0.87	2.36	1.04	2.36	1.05	2.23	1.03
Use of bibliography	1.97	1.04	2.36	1.20	2.59	1.04	1.65	0.83	1.35	0.78

*Respondents responded to the statement "Editors and reviewers of manuscripts base their decisions of the acceptability of manuscripts on a variety of criteria—please indicate the importance of the following criteria as they relate to your journal." The weightings: 5=of most importance; 4=of great importance; 3=of average importance; 2=of less importance; and 1=of least importance.

Table II

CONTENT CRITERIA FOR MANUSCRIPT ACCEPTABILITY

Criteria	Total x̄	Total S.D.	Research x̄	Research S.D.	Scholarly x̄	Scholarly S.D.	Professional x̄	Professional S.D.	Association x̄	Association S.D.
Interest to readers	4.55	0.56	4.08	0.28	4.45	0.65	4.65	0.51	4.71	0.46
Applicability to practical or applied problems in the field	4.34	0.80	4.25	0.75	4.21	0.88	4.42	0.81	4.40	0.68
Timeliness of topic	4.33	0.73	3.83	0.83	4.27	0.73	4.48	0.60	4.28	0.86
Originality	3.87	0.93	3.91	0.79	4.02	0.79	3.74	1.04	3.94	0.93
Anticipatory of problems or issues in the field	3.72	1.00	3.16	0.93	3.97	1.02	3.69	0.91	3.68	1.15
Discussion of educational issues	3.71	1.08	2.91	1.16	3.86	1.08	3.74	1.08	3.83	0.85
Contribution to basic knowledge	3.61	1.03	4.08	0.90	3.91	1.02	3.22	1.03	3.83	0.78
Good Taste	3.53	0.97	3.09	0.83	3.51	1.01	3.49	0.96	4.00	0.90
Depth	3.48	0.91	3.83	0.93	3.70	0.90	3.34	0.90	3.22	0.87
Professional controversiality of topic	3.32	1.08	2.75	0.86	3.47	1.08	3.25	1.08	3.57	1.12
Of long term definitive value	3.27	1.08	4.00	0.89	3.59	1.23	2.94	0.91	3.11	0.96
Contribution to education as a field of study	3.25	1.17	4.16	1.03	3.27	1.26	3.00	1.10	3.38	1.03
Breadth	3.17	0.80	3.08	0.99	3.40	0.72	3.07	0.81	3.05	0.80
Discussion of data implications	3.15	1.13	3.83	0.71	3.62	1.08	2.70	1.11	3.00	0.97
Orientation to general rather than specialized readership	3.14	1.17	2.50	1.08	3.10	1.17	3.17	1.15	3.55	1.19
Based on current research in field or research tradition	3.10	0.99	3.83	0.83	3.35	0.85	2.72	1.04	3.16	0.78
Policy oriented (position paper)	2.99	1.08	3.00	0.77	3.45	1.12	2.68	0.99	2.88	1.18
Value oriented (opinion pieces)	2.95	1.01	2.45	1.03	3.10	1.07	2.94	0.98	2.94	0.93
Social controversy surrounding topic	2.79	1.02	2.54	0.82	2.75	1.21	2.84	0.89	2.88	1.13
Descriptive orientation	2.66	1.04	2.00	0.85	2.64	1.13	2.69	0.98	3.05	0.99
Of interest to education professors	2.60	1.21	3.16	0.93	2.86	1.08	2.25	1.18	2.66	1.49
Theoretical orientation	2.52	1.09	3.41	0.90	2.91	1.16	2.05	0.81	2.44	1.19
Data presented with limited discussion of implications	2.29	1.05	2.50	1.16	2.24	0.98	2.25	1.04	2.38	1.19

The Research Journal

Research journal editors rate the following process criteria as most important: the appropriate use of statistics, the appropriateness of a manuscript's total organization, the validity of logic used, and the clarity and conciseness of writing. There is also some concern that papers be theoretically grounded and be compatible with the ethics inherent in the disciplines extended in the manuscripts.

It is of interest that those higher-rated items that address the notion of a "community of scholars" refer to standardization rather than the celebration of the ideas of colleagues or even uncovering one's fallibility, given possible alternative perspectives on one's work. Thus, replicability and the use of standard empirical methodologies are more important components than suggestions for future research, alternative interpretations of data, and the quality of literature reviews and bibliography.

Turning to content criteria, editors choose papers that they believe are applicable to practical problems, are of long-term definitive value, and are of interest to their readers. These papers should contribute to education as a field of study and to basic knowledge. In fact, the balance is on a manuscript's value to scholarship. A paper is judged primarily on methodological criteria, under the assumption that good research should be used; it is applicable because it is valid knowledge. Editors and reviewers for research journals examine papers for their rigor.

There is research on the research that is published, asking whether standards are being maintained and what the cost of such watchfulness might be. The research on research takes three basic lines, distinguished by whether fault-finding is a prelude to calls for greater rigor, whether the author believes there are systemic problems with educational research that require serious discussion, or whether the systemic problems invalidate the value of positivistic knowledge or if its procedures need drastic overhaul.

Ward, Hall, and Schramm (1975) represent the first strain. A sample of 121 published research papers were selected from a population of 1,486 from 44 research journals and re-reviewed on 33 characteristics. These items included the following: hypotheses are clearly stated; important terms are defined; relationship of the problem to previous research is made clear; the population and sample are described; tables and illustrations are effectively used; conclusions are significant; and the tone of the report displays an unbiased, impartial, scientific attitude. They found that, "For all journals, only 8% of the research articles were rated 'acceptable as is for publication,' 31% were rated 'acceptable after minor revisions,' 34% were rated 'acceptable only after major revisions,' and 27% were rated 'reject'" (p. 118).

Shaver and Norton (1980) represent the second line in their examination of random sampling and replication of papers that appeared over a ten-year period in the *American Educational Research Journal.* They note, "The lack of random assignment makes the use of inferential statistics suspect, and the failure to eliminate the effects of extraneous variables through randomization presents serious threats to internal validity. . . .And our data indicate that replications are reported even more infrequently than is random sampling" (p. 14).

Mahoney (1976), with a more specific attack, concerned that only positive results are published, representing the third approach, suggests changing the game rules for publication, by, for example, evaluating manuscripts "solely on the basis of their relevance and their methodology" (p. 105) and not merely on the statistical significance of their results and their apparent formal correctness.

These three approaches, suggesting the need either for greater rigor, debate or reform, have the potential to change procedures and reviewing criteria; but it is doubtful that they will, in fact, have this effect unless authors act through their professional associations to support positions that they believe to be productive.

The Scholarly Journal

Editors of scholarly journals in education are more interested than their research editor counterparts in an author's clarity, conciseness, and spirited style of writing and less interested in an author's emotional neutrality, appropriate use of statistics, and a study's replicability. A paper need not have an experimental design. The author's "track record" looms, in comparison, as more important, though it is not of great significance.

Regarding content criteria, these editors are most concerned that the topic be of interest to readers, that it be timely, applicable to current and anticipated problems, and original. Depth and breadth are of about equal importance, and there is an interest in a paper's controversiality and orientation to a general audience. There seems to be an interest in balancing the research qualities of a paper with its professional value.

There is a "reflexive" literature on the scholarly article, as there is on the research article. This literature takes two forms: first, exploratory investigations of the relationship between usefulness and specific qualities of scholarship and, second, ideologically based advocacy of alternatives to positivistic knowledge.

The most telling work has dealt with service-oriented professionals outside education and their use of the social and behavioral science knowledge. The education community is discovering the problem of "how to generate a conscious sensitivity among those who create and use research. . . . Practitioners and scholars must inquire together to discover research modes that most productively serve the massive problems" (Schubert, 1980, p. 23). Scholars in the social and behavioral sciences are advancing our understanding.

Rothman (1980), for example, examined how an organization's structure and climate affect research utilization and how the research process and the resulting report affect use. Rothman suggests that useful research is supported by top leadership, shows awareness of the resource base of a client system, is mindful of how an organization works, relates affirmatively to organizational members, and suggests directions that minimize threat. There are scores of other suggestions.

Another scholar of the meaning of scholarship, Carol Weiss (1980b), finds, "By and large, officials value research not only for the specific data it provides but more importantly for its *ideas*. It is the generalizations and concepts from the social sciences that they often find most useful in helping them construct their images of their mission" (p. 269). She examines the relationship between utility and research: quality, conformity with user expectations, challenge to the status quo, and action orientation are significantly related to "use".

The second, more hortatory approach, challenges the assumptions of analytic science and suggests alternative criteria for a science that has utility. Argyris (1970) likens analytic science, the fuel of research journals, to an authoritarian system of production, while his alternative, organic science, is more respecting of human subjects and users.

These are but a few examples of a growing literature on the applicability of knowledge. Although it is unlikely that many gatekeepers are familiar with this scholarship, an author's attention to it is likely to bring into focus criteria that scholarly editors deem important.

The Professional Journal

Editors of professional journals have the narrowest range of process criteria scores among the journal types. Writing quality and organization are important, and data and statistical-related items receive low marks. There is limited concern with an author's use of literature and relatively more interest in the reputation of an author and his or her institution. One has the impression that process-related notions are not very critical.

The focus is on content, on its interest to readers and its applicability to practical problems. Timeliness is important and is more critical than originality. As for process items, it is difficult to discern biases as measured by a paper's relation to current research, policy issues, value significance, descriptive or theoretical orientation, or controversiality. It is not important that a paper interest the professoriate.

Commissioning much of what they publish, either directly or through the selection of guest editors, editors of professional education journals are distinguished from their counterparts in all other categories in that they do not have referents outside themselves—not a research methodology or a theory/practice interest or the representation of an educational association's priorities. Timeliness, reader interest, and applicable value, as editors define these criteria, are by themselves most critical. The best advice to an author is to know the editor's view of education and to be acquainted with the actual, rather than the potential, issues educators confront.

The literature on writing in this area is represented by the many books designed to assist professionals to write more effectively. A particularly good source is Ewing's *Writing for Results in Business, Government, and the Professions* (1974). Ewing advises authors on how to decide whether to write, to get off to the right start, to learn strategies of persuasion, to organize facts and ideas, to make a convincing written analysis, to use an appropriate presentation pattern, to create the right tone in a paper. The advice is sound and down to earth. Ewing concludes, "Writing for results is not an art form, not a literary technique. It is an act of understanding ideas and people in relationship. The secret of success is somewhat like that of a wiley old golfer I used to know. He had an uncanny ability to win tournaments, and people used to ask him what was the secret of his swing. 'Secret's not in my swing,' he used to answer. 'It's in what I know about the course'" (p. 425).

The Association Journal

Given the newswriting background of many association journal gatekeepers, it is not surprising that clarity and conciseness of writing and spirited style loom as large as they do. Because these journals serve a public relations function, their editors are sensitive to author or institutional reputation. There is a concern that statistics be used appropriately, but statistics have descriptive, not inferential, value.

Among content criteria, reader interest is important, with the readership described as generalists. Descriptive papers that are in good taste, timely, original, and that have applicable value are preferred. Association journal editors, more than their professional journal counterparts, keep in mind the interests of the professoriate as readers and believe that articles should contribute to education as a field of study. This, no doubt, stems from a lobbying orientation.

Quality writing, with simple exposition and an absence of jargon, is sought in educational news and feature writing. The literature on writing in this area has less a "how-to" orientation and more an urgent intent to prepare newswriters who are skilled in reporting scientific and educational activities. Editors expect reporters to ask the right questions, to compose more than a "mindless retailing of information" (Dixon, 1980, p. 219), to avoid premature publicity, to seek informants who are credible spokespersons, and to develop an understanding of the institution about which they are reporting.

Farago (1976) admonishes science writers "to establish a nexus with the reader. . .of generating some sense of personal participation" (p. 11). Like the education writer, "the science journalist is caught between opposing forces" (p. 50), the reader and the subject, and must balance the two interests. "The best science writing is committed to a point of view that includes not only science but also society. . . .Such writing succeeds in establishing contact with the public through emotional sincerity rather than semantic accuracy expressed in pedantic lists of facts and definitions. . . .Science must be regarded as exemplary material, for the arbiter of history is man and not the other way round" (p. 51). This same spirit permeates the world of the education writer whose focus is the association journal.

Criteria Related to Form of Inquiry

As previously discussed, editors provide varying amounts and different kinds of information to referees regarding the criteria they ought to use in critiquing manuscripts. Some editors simply request that referees provide their best judgment; others supply detailed forms with explicit instructions. An example is included in the Appendix.

Often, the referee is asked to react to a subset of the criteria noted in Tables I and II. Reactions are sought regarding a paper's quality of writing, topic, length in relation to purpose, originality, and appropriateness to the journal's readers. Less often proposed are detailed criteria that are contingent on the form of scholarship, such as theory development, reviews of the field, case studies, and technological developments. For example, a case study might require a sufficient delineation of the setting and situation of the actors and the generalizability of case findings, among other dimensions. A theory development manuscript might require an appropriate examination of authors' assumptions and presuppositions, definitions of terms, and the propositions' relation to other world views. A paper describing a technological development might require pilot testing for the innovation, indicators of cost and complexity of implementation, and evaluation data. Obviously, it makes good sense to be aware of the criteria that are specific to a journal and to the type of manuscript presented. If criteria are not published in the journal, authors should request them from editors.

Reasons for Rejection

Many papers are returned without benefit of external review because they are incongruent with journal type or the directions taken by specific gatekeepers. Once manuscripts enter the competition for space, referees judge them on the criteria alluded to above. Although there is a kind of impersonal objectivity connoted by lists and statistics, each referee interprets the criteria based on personal knowledge, experience, and expectations. For example, many journals ask referees to judge the value of a paper for the publication's readership. On what basis do the referees truly know the cognitive and experiential characteristics of the readers and the reasons they read the articles? It is likely that a good deal of subjectivity will be evident in such a judgment.

The editors who were surveyed in my study of acceptance criteria (Silverman, 1978) were asked the major reasons papers were rejected. The 130 editors provided 232 reasons, 121 suggesting poor writing or technical execution and 82 indicating unsuitability for the readership. Research journal editors address primarily the more technical dimensions—weak rationale and inadequate methodological design. Scholarly journal editors remark on the poor quality of scholarship and writing as well as lack of relevance for the readership, with a somewhat greater concern for the latter. For example, scholarly journal editors note that the style is often deficient and the material is of inadequate scope for the readers' interests. In addition, they emphasize that fresh views are absent, judged against *their* previously published material or knowledge in general.

Editors of professional journals are concerned about technical and writing qualities but interpret these interests differently. They do not accept papers that are obscure, loaded with jargon, and of limited value to practitioners who are attempting to cope with crises. They are ill disposed toward manuscripts that are thinly disguised dissertations and only a bit more generous toward a former speech.

Association gatekeepers, though concerned about writing quality, also return papers that do not conform to the needs and purposes of the association or readership as they have identified them.

Few journals are overwhelmed with manuscripts of the quality desired, and few are not overwhelmed with manuscripts of varying quality and suitability. Although most authors invest themselves in their contributions, the crush of papers often finds the editor taking an instrumental, unempathic attitude toward any one manuscript. There operates a sort of Darwinian mentality which is buffered by the need to have a sufficient amount of material to maintain subscription commitments.

Though we expect a paper's probability of acceptance to be improved through the author's attention to the strategic and tactical considerations addressed in this book, authors must learn to live with rejection. We will examine this concern in the following chapter.

Part III
AFTER THE VERDICT

Following the editor's decision and the receipt of the letter, opened "with pounding heart and trembling fingers," the author will experience one of a number of possible emotions—joy, anger, self-doubt—to name but a few. Though most authors ask that the decision letter be sent to their offices, it is not unusual for them to request home delivery. Why share possible bad news with secretaries and colleagues whose eyes roam over adjacent mailboxes?

Although it is impossible to eliminate the soul-searching that follows the rejection of a manuscript or a request for extensive revision, authors should understand that even those whom they would identify as "successful" have had their share of denials. Of course, 10 to 20 percent of submitted manuscripts are accepted, often after revision. Given this, the author must be concerned about appropriate rights and responsibilities as they pertain to the accepted manuscript and journal relationships.

The chapters in this section will assist authors to cope with the editorial decision and will examine authors' rights and responsibilities.

Chapter 6
HANDLING THE REACTION

ACCEPTANCE

Look Ma, No Hands

A marvellous sense of accomplishment accompanies the acceptance of a manuscript: one's contribution is deemed to be of value to others. Though "acceptance" carries reward implications for most and promises survival for some, the symbolic acts of gift giving and receiving provide the real meaning: publish or perish as a member of an extended community whose members grow through each others' offices.

The author's obligations in the publishing process continue after the flush of victory and its expression—through excessive humility or semipublic announcement—which make one's students proud and spur one's colleagues to renew their publishing efforts, if not to cope with a barely concealed jealousy. What should the author expect?

Style

It is common for manuscripts to require minor to extensive revision to bring them into conformity with the stylistic conventions of the journals. As noted earlier, editors differ in their insistence that papers, as submitted, reflect the manuscript style expected in the finished product. On such points as systematic literature citation, construction of tables, and usage of conventional symbols, some education journal editors refer authors to their own house styles and others to the guidelines of, for example, the Modern Language Association, the American Psychological Association, or the University of Chicago Press.

Some editors dissuade authors from using footnotes under the assumption that if material is not sufficiently important for the text it should be eliminated. Other editors promote the use of footnotes as an economical method of publishing material of interest to a segment of the readership or to give a manuscript a dialogical quality. Authors may be asked to place some material in an appendix both to supplement the text and to reduce the need for readers to request matter related to methodology. Full or partial survey instruments, operationalizations of variables, and tables presenting complex statistical matter can usefully appear as appendices. Such material not only assists the reader in understanding the author's procedures and the interpretations based on their use but also comprises an act of community: the author shares his or her assumptions and judgments.

An important style-related matter that typically requires attention is the abstract. Journals that use abstracts usually request 50 to 100 words summarizing the article—its topic and questions, methodology, and conclusions. A concise summary is important to the reader with limited time, who scans abstracts to determine whether an article promises to address an interest.

The less traditional the paper, the more difficult the abstract is to develop. Scholarly, as opposed to research, knowledge, and issue examinations, require creative efforts to capture their meaning and value in a few words. Although abstracts should not contain material that is not supported in the article, they can do more than summarize if an editor so wishes. For example, editors who realize that their journals are in competition with others for reader attention may favor abstracts that "hook" the reader by using provocative statements. Some abstracts legitimate or celebrate the author.

The author should pay close attention to the title and might suggest that the editor use a specific "running head" at the top of each page if the journal uses them. Key words are used in information storage systems to code a published manuscript and to allow for its appropriate retrieval. An article's potential value is greatly expanded through its inclusion in secondary information systems, such as abstract services. Authors should assist editors by writing precise abstracts and designating key words upon which further use will depend.

The final style-related item we will discuss is the creation of graphs and charts. Journals usually provide instructions for "artwork" preparation, and though some allow the publication of typed or hand-drawn work, most require that illustration material be professionally rendered. Qualified draftspersons are available on most campuses in teaching aids laboratories, engineering departments, and printing offices. Many journals have access to artists who will perform the work and bill the author directly for it.

Tune-up

The author should insure that any minor, self-initiated revisions be made prior to the setting of the manuscript into type. Authors will reap more than unkind words from the editor if revisions are made at the galley stage; they will be charged for alterations over a small minimum. The insertion or deletion of just a few words may require the resetting of an entire paragraph, and thus costs can escalate quickly. There are some authors who find it difficult to alter even one word of an initial draft and others who revise and update extensively at every turn. Unless the former are "natural" writers, they are unlikely to receive acceptance letters, and the latter court the possibility of not receiving future ones.

Clearly, writers believe that their creations are important, but editors do not expect that egoism will prevail at the expense of attention to other authors or good relations with printers. Editors carefully measure manuscripts to reflect total space requirements. Revisions that lengthen or shorten a manuscript create obvious problems.

If an author intends to alter the manuscript in any way, this intention should be communicated to the editor when the manuscript is accepted. The editor will then have an opportunity to indicate the amount of time available to the author for making the modifications.

Did I Say That?

If the editor does not tell the author that galley proofs will be available for inspection, the author should request them. Although editors and copy editors attempt to avoid doing violence to a paper and usually request author approval of major wording changes and deletions, infelicitious editorial modifications may bypass the author. Writers are usually not surprised or troubled by minor changes; such is not the case if bad mistakes are made by a less-than-competent or distracted copy editor. An example of an indefensible error was made on a manuscript written by a colleague of mine: the word "socializing" replaced "socialization," not once but many times. Had the galleys not been inspected, the author would have earned an interesting reputation.

The author should read the galley proofs deliberately, more than once, with a break between readings. Words and statistics should be compared with the manuscript copy to insure that all is included. Of course the author is also interested in detecting common compositional errors such as misspellings. Some authors take pride in using printer's symbols to communicate with the copy editor. In neophytes' hands, such symbols may obfuscate more than elucidate. The copy editor might prefer the use of ordinary English to describe the problems.

Above all, the author should return the corrected proofs within the time specified by the editor—often no longer than 72 hours after their arrival in the author's hands. Thus, authors should keep the editorial office, as well as their own secretaries, apprised of their addresses if temporarily away from the office.

Printers run on very tight schedules and inform the editor when galleys should be returned. A delay of even one day can mean that the journal issue is put back, not one day, but one week or even several weeks. The issue may go to "the end of the line." Since editorial offices are aware of this policy, they will not wait for authors who are slow in picking up their mail or acting on it.

The Tenure Committee Needs To Know

Unless a manuscript is "rounding out an issue" or is part of a special number, the editor is unlikely to inform the author of when the paper is scheduled for publication. The editor is not acting irresponsibly. It is likely that the accepted papers have not been measured for length or put in final form, that book reviews and other features have not been received and their space requirements assessed, and that the foci of issues have yet to be decided.

Many editors attempt to group papers that have some relationship, though the combination may not be called a "special issue" and the connections may not even be made explicit by the editor. Such placement, it should be noted, allows for the exercise of an editor's creativity and subsequent judgments of his or her work.

For example, backing a paper on attrition with one on faculty development suggests a connection different from backing it with one on finance.

The author is likely to disseminate copies of the accepted manuscript, before publication, to colleagues who may want to cite it in their work. Promotion and tenure and graduate committees may want assurances that an accepted manuscript will be used. A publishing date suggests a high degree of certainty. For these reasons, if not for general interest, it is appropriate for authors to request that they be kept informed about the likely publication date and the planned date when the scheduling decision is made.

Complimentary Copies and Reprints

Each journal has a policy regarding the number of complimentary journal copies or reprints it sends to authors. There seems to be little uniformity: some send two journal copies, others six, and others fifty article reprints. The publisher will inform the author of journal policy at the time the manuscript is accepted. At this time the author will also learn when to order additional reprints.

The quality of reprints varies. Some are executed by the printer as an overrun; others are done by the publisher on copying equipment; some have elegant cover pages; others none. Regardless, they tend to be expensive, though the unit cost decreases with the number purchased. Authors should recognize the vanity-serving function of reprints and should order a number they truly believe they will need.

There is a tradition in the natural sciences that has transferred to the behavioral sciences—the use of a specially imprinted postcard sent by readers to request reprints from authors. Packets of such cards regularly accompany scholars when they use library copies of journals. The less traditionally analytic the readership, the less likely reprints will be requested—and needed.

What Am I Signing Away?

As a result of new copyright regulations, most publishers ask authors to sign copyright agreements. We will examine them in the next chapter and mention them here only because the author is likely to receive one with an acceptance letter. An agreement should specify each party's responsibilities and, like the manuscript, should be written in clear English.

To Revise or Not to Revise

Authors should recognize that a very large percentage of manuscripts that are adequately revised in response to the editor's and referees' suggestions are eventually accepted. In fact, if the editor does not believe that a manuscript is revisable by the author and of interest to the readership, it is unlikely that recommendations on revision would be made.

Unless the author finds the suggested modifications to be onerous or inappropriate, the journal that promises acceptance after adequate revision should not be abandoned. It might take some time to locate another potential publisher; and by then, the paper may be out of date. The author should understand that the journal has already committed a good deal of resources to the reviewing of a paper, and it is unlikely that a large backlog of papers await publication. The writer should not allow the ego to interfere by supporting the drift to another publisher. The author should have an interest in being published, not in being stroked.

It goes without saying that editors and reviewers can err in their criticisms of a manuscript. If the recommendations on revision are debatable, the author can reply to the referees, with the editor acting as an intermediary between the parties. An author can also request that another reviewer examine certain aspects of the paper. Editors often comply. Obviously, the author's reply should be intelligently and forcefully supported and any judgments as to the competency of the reviewers avoided.

It often happens that editors receive second drafts with letters from authors noting that the reviewers' suggestions have informed the revision. Upon examination of the draft the editor finds, however, that few of the observations have been incorporated in the new paper or that the changes have been executed in as superficial a way as possible. Modifications are superimposed on the original, or retyping masks an absence of change. The pointlessness of such an exercise should be obvious.

Since editors expect "good will" for all parties to the review process, the suggestion of cheating will likely elicit an angry reaction, placing the author under the added burden of not being trusted. This exchange is typically culminated when the author sends a letter offering apologies, doing little for his or her self-concept.

If in the author's view the suggested changes are inappropriate or onerous, ...other journal ought to be considered. However, editors often concur in their perceptions regarding weaknesses in a manuscript, and the more objective the problem, such as low response rate to a survey, the more likely there will be agreement. It should also be noted that reviewers read for more than one journal. Thus, a reviewer may tell an editor that a paper under review has not been modified since a previous submission to, and rejection by, another journal. Although editors expect many submissions to have had histories elsewhere, a more critical eye and less generous feelings are taken toward papers that are known to have been simply popped into an envelope after a previous rejection.

Depending on the nature and extent of the problems that authors correct, editors may alone judge the adequacy of the revision or they may return the manuscript to the original reviewers to determine the adequacy of the modifications. Most authors would rather the editor make the judgment—to expedite the process and, perhaps, to take advantage of the editor's lack of expertise in a specific area.

It is not uncommon for subsequent reviews of a paper to turn up problems that were not identified in earlier readings, especially if a new reviewer is consulted on the revision. Some, of course, would judge the inclusion of a new party at this stage of the review process as unethical. Oversights by the editor or reviewer in the initial review may be detected in the second pass, and although many editors will overlook the errors at this point, some do insist that additional modifications be made. Authors usually do not challenge the new requests, being as dependent as they are and also concerned about the excellence of their papers.

It is difficult to advise authors on how to react to oversights unless the nature of the manuscript problem is taken into account. Thus, one must rely on the simple notion that it does not pay to fight with the editor. The editor will be sensitive to his or her error and is likely to grow from the experience.

The manuscript revision process can be a significant learning experience if the author welcomes it as an opportunity to sharpen his or her work. The norms and values, if not the direction of an area, are evident in the communication patterns, and the exchange can allow an author to better understand the structure. Such an appreciation is critical for personal success as well as area growth. Whether one likes it or not, the reactions one receives during the review process are probably the most honest feedback one can hope for as a professional.

WE REGRET TO INFORM YOU

Although papers, not authors, are rejected, it is not likely that the author will keep this distinction in mind at the time the rejection letter arrives. More likely responses include anger directed at the editor, a vow to succeed with another publication, and, the most insidious, self-doubt.

To Try Again

Editors would rather accept than "fail to use" a manuscript. It is more fulfilling to participate in a colleague's success than to lengthen an ever-growing list of resentful authors. Neither authors nor editors enjoy the double levels operating when they interact in contexts outside of the journal; it is always more difficult when their history has not been a positive one.

The important first step for authors whose work is not accepted is to understand why the decision was reached. Understanding should be sought on a variety of levels. If the editor has not supplied sufficient or persuasive information regarding the causes of the judgment, it should be requested. On another level, the author should ask himself or herself why the manuscript evidenced the problems uncovered and how they might be avoided in the future—not by not writing another paper but through the development of new skills or understandings. Every professional action in which we engage has personal meanings. They must be considered in combination if we are to grow.

The author may believe a manuscript can be resurrected even though the editor has not formally invited another draft. It is appropriate to write to the editor indicating one's intention to submit a revision and the reasons for the renewed effort. Editors will be more receptive to the arguments, and the revision, the softer or the more "subjective" were the referees' judgments. It may not be possible to correct a low response rate, but a poorly written paper can be rewritten with the assistance of an accomplished editor, or a literature base can be more fully developed and used.

Resubmission, even if not requested, will typically prompt the editor to review the previous effort and the correspondence regarding it. The revision and the transmittal letter, if "persuasive," will suggest a commitment that editors tend to find positive, and if the paper seems to be improved, another chance for acceptance will be offered.

I'll Show You

Should the author decide to send the work elsewhere, the choice of journal ought to be informed by the many considerations treated elsewhere in this book, along with the reactions to the previous effort.

The paper should not simply be recopied and mailed. It will need to be refashioned for the next publication; and if the originally perceived problems are not dealt with through revision, the author's choices should be more fully and persuasively explained. An interim period for reflective judgment and possible modification can be valuable. The decisions one makes at this point require a dispassionate attitude.

Of course, the paper may not be usable, and it might best be buried. If the author has thoughtfully considered the significance of the experience, the rejection may have greater career value than the acceptance of a paper that, for whatever reasons, is celebrated with its faults or praised for the wrong reasons.

Who Am I?

Many editors are sensitive to the psychological impact of manuscript rejection on an author, and they attempt to soften the blow through the way they "fail to use" a work. Nevertheless, comparison with successfully published colleagues is inevitable. One examines the journal and finds work of questionable quality; one smiles somewhat falsely when a colleague shoves an acceptance letter in one's face. Worse, the author becomes masochistic, reveling in rejection. This reaction, though not pervasive, is clearly evident in those authors who in their letters to editors seem to enjoy the significance their topic or method does not have. Their value is that they are not valued.

Editors may be concerned about the person behind the manuscript. Regardless, authors need to support themselves at the same time they learn from negative experiences. Such a foundation will undergird future success.

Chapter 7
ETHICAL AND LEGAL CONSIDERATIONS

Ethical and legal considerations are of greatest concern to the author during the early stages of knowledge development: during inquiry and the development of the initial draft of the manuscript. Such considerations also pertain, however, to the later stages of the dissemination process, which are the subject of this book.

Some of the issues are complex and not well appreciated by authors until they are brought to their attention. This is especially so regarding copyright laws and procedures. Authors and publishers have both rights and responsibilities that are not apparent to the uninitiated. Some of them are noted in the final section of this chapter.

Certain of the concerns are grounded in statute and court interpretation, but many are based on time-worn, common-sense principles—notions that should be part of the normal development of educated people. Editors react to author behavior that falls above as well as below common expectations and often discuss among themselves examples in the latter category.

One side of the behavior continuum is represented by the scrupulous author who, after having had his manuscript accepted, asked the editor to withdraw it if a sentence that might be construed as too critical of a colleague could not be softened. There are more examples that fall on the other side of the continuum. Of questionable "value" is the appearance of the same paper in two journals, with each printing showing a different coauthor, title, and introductory and concluding paragraphs; an author's attempt to convince an editor that an original typescript has been submitted by reproducing one copy on bond and two copies on low-grade copy paper; a senior author's deletion of a second author's name, without this person's approval, on the revision of a manuscript; and an author's certification that an accepted paper has not been previously used, only for the editor to see it in another journal published within a week after receiving the author's letter.

Every editor has such stories, and they often pertain to authors who have very significant reputations. As gatekeeper, the editor often feels a responsibility to judge the ethics of publishing as well as the content of manuscripts. However, the editor's role, as both formally defined and self-defined, determines the action the editor may take in response to a breach of ethics. Depending on the editor's status, tenure, and relation to the publisher's agenda, among other factors, unethical behavior can be ignored or confronted, either directly by responding to the author or indirectly by being less sympathetic to an author's future initiatives.

The ethics involved in publishing are based, by and large, on the same principles that inform behavior in other situations. The issues treated below may not pertain to an author's specific problem; common decency will usually yield a solution, but if one is in doubt, it is certainly appropriate to request advice from the journal editor.

Authorship

The first page of the manuscript lists the names and institutional affiliations of the author or authors; in other words, who is to get credit. Coauthors generally determine before submission who is to be ranked as the first, or senior, author of a manuscript. The editor does not have any responsibility to question the decision unless it is modified during the review process. Through many revisions accomplished by one author, it is clearly possible for the order of authors' names to change. The editor typically corresponds with but one of the authors, who assumes the responsibility for negotiating the acceptance of the manuscript. The editor welcomes proof that the other authors have received copies of all correspondence.

The question of crediting institutions arises when an author moves from one setting to another before or about the time an article appears. Authors often want to begin their new institutional affiliation on a high note—why credit the college that refused tenure or failed to match the new offer? The norm, however, is that all institutions related to an author's work should be cited appropriately. If an author wrote a paper while at institution X and published it while at institution Y, this should be noted.

Authors take advantage of institutional settings in ways other than as users of lights, heat, and phones. In educatic.. articles we frequently comment on institutional behavior, actions within the organizations of employment and those in which we work in other capacities, for example, as consultants. How should an author deal with a study that discusses ways in which a college administration succeeded in defeating an attempt to organize faculty into a collective bargaining unit? Does an author or journal have the right to publish work that can have a direct impact on institutional fortunes? Only a good impact? Should the author receive permission to publish such a paper? If so, from whom? Is it a proper concern of an editor that the author be aware of the risks to self and institution created by the publication of a paper? Is the editor only concerned with such risks if the manuscript is commissioned? Does it matter whether the paper was written before the editor expressed an interest? Should the author conceal the institution's name and location if the data may have harmful consequences? Is it, in fact, possible to conceal the identity of an institution? Does it make a difference if a finger is pointed at personal rather than institutional inadequacies?

Editors approach the use of data on specific institutions differently according to their personal makeup and the type of journal they represent. There is no common set of principles, though some editors might attempt to develop them. It is important for authors to address, in transmittal letters, legitimate questions regarding the ethics involved in data collection and use. One such question is whether the work has been approved by a human subjects review panel, when appropriate.

This is not to suggest that authors conform to institutional expectations if they intend to publish, nor that editors not use their publications for exposé. It is simply suggested that authors address explicitly the rules they have employed and allow the editor to react to the actual, rather than the implied, conditions undergirding the manuscript.

The final author-related issue we will discuss concerns the publication of a manuscript for its direct entreprenurial value to the author. Scholars may perish if they do not publish; consultants may languish without clients. Journals are used to serve pocketbooks, and although many editors decry this state of affairs, they also realize that genuine communication interests are insufficiently strong to keep publications publishing.

Authors' benefits ought to be derivative, not central. For example, the introduction of an educational technology ought to be based on sound pilot and evaluative data and not published prematurely. Language, in addition to being clear, should reflect appropriate adjectives that are not stronger than they should be, and writers ought to be conscious of the metaphoric qualities of their words.

A writer ought to be explicit enough about the scope and depth of his or her experience that potential buyers can assess the reliability of the product. At times authors' explicit or implicit expertise is laughable; and if it were not for some journals' need to publish "experts," there might be greater understanding and less hype in published work. Too many authors capture and label an idea whose time has come or lobby a theory that seems to respond to education issues and "milk" it for audiences needing to confirm beliefs or to lean on a higher rationale for action. There are too many snake oil merchants who hawk their panaceas or intone their catechisms.

Sacrifice for something larger than self is not prevalent in these days when we have apotheosized me-ism. All parties—authors, editors, and readers—have a role to play in insuring that goals larger than self-promotion are served in the publishing process.

Scholarship

Authors need to be reminded that they often unwittingly use others' work without sufficient attribution. Important works, over time, become part of us; on the other hand, some writers simply do not know how to paraphrase or cite sources. The skills necessary for the appropriate use of others' materials are most highly developed among authors of traditional research papers, but they are required as well of authors of all types of manuscripts. Authors should ask themselves what the roots of their manuscripts are—whether ideas or published work—and cite them in the reference section or in footnotes. Certainly tracing the practice and intellectual networks in which our work is embedded will counter the me-ism mentioned above.

Of course, authors often cite themselves. In one case, an author cited his previous article, which cited an earlier paper, and it an even earlier one. There we1~ at least four uses of the same idea that had not changed over the years. The notion was not powerful or recent, yet it appeared to be. Is this unethical in spirit if not in fact?

Editors are primarily concerned with authors' prior and subsequent use of articles published in their journals. They expect to be informed about other uses and to receive requests from, and to give permission to, other publishers. Editors differ in their willingness to use material that has appeared elsewhere and to allow their journal's content to be republished. For the research journal editor, it is likely that one printing will be perceived as sufficient; for the professional and association journal editor, subsequent republication is usually desirable, and work that first appeared elsewhere is welcome. The scholarly journal editor is literally in the middle. He or she will reprint, or allow to be republished elsewhere, work that is directed to different readerships. How different "different" is is, of course, debatable, with authors tending to maximize, and editors tending to minimize, the variation.

Requests by authors for permission to use their own material in subsequent collections or in a book tend to be granted by editors as a matter of course. Others who want to include a work in an edited volume are typically charged a small fee, which may be divided between the journal and the author. Authors typically have the right of approval over such republishing.

Of course, appropriate citations of initial publication must be made in all cases, and journals may have special requirements as to how the reference is to read.

The Contract

Many publishers accompany their letters of acceptance with contracts by which authors transfer some of their rights in return for certain benefits. Authors may be required to verify that the accepted manuscript has not been used in whole or in part in any other publication without the current publisher's knowledge and to agree not to use the work again without approval. The journal publisher will provide maximum protection for the author by registering the article with the U.S. Copyright Office and by requiring that other persons in the field may use the material, in acceptable way, only after they have obtained permission and agreed to pay any applicable fee. A sample publishing agreement is included in Appendix C.

Journals, typically operating as non-profit entities, invest the equivalent of many dollars in personnel time in the adjudication and editing of manuscripts, in addition to paying production and other operating costs, which are themselves often not covered by subscription revenue. Given this investment, journals expect others who use their "property," and who will benefit commercially or otherwise from republishing the material, to help offset the original costs.

The Copyright Act of 1976, which went into effect in 1978, is complex and is itself the subject of books and monographs in which certain sections of the law are explicated for the general reader or for specific users, such as publishers (Thatcher, 1977). Readers who are particularly interested in such details as copyright protection as it relates to translations or classroom use of published material are encouraged to consult the *Copyright Handbook* (Johnston, 1978).

Regardless of special interests, all authors should understand that copyright only protects what they have created "in tangible form sufficiently permanent to permit it to be communicated for a period of more than transitory duration. . ." (Johnston, 1978, p. 14). For a manuscript, it is the words, not the ideas, that are protected. There may be ethical-professional injunctions against using others' ideas, but; "In no case does copyright protection for an original work of authorship extend to any idea, procedure, process, system, method of operation, concept, principle, or discovery, regardless of the form in which it is described, explained, illustrated, or embodied in such work" (Johnston, 1978, p. 133). In fact, "there are two other exclusions—a 'fact' and 'news'—that are not expressly mentioned. . ." (Johnston, 1978, p. 18).

Authors should take reasonable care that only trustworthy persons review their manuscripts before submission. In fact, it probably would be wise to share one's work with more than one colleague to assure corroboration in the event that one's role in developing an idea is challenged. Certainly, authors should expect referees not to use any portion of the work they critique. Should one determine that this injunction has not been maintained, the author should use the available professional networks to deal with the problem.

Concluding Comment

Publishing in education is a process rather than a discrete act. A published paper is backed by the author's deliberation in all phases of the process, from assessing the motives of the work and their congruence with the roles of the various types of education journals, to becoming aware of the specific directions taken by journals within one of the types, to developing an appropriate paper and critiquing it in view of the requirements of a potential publisher, to submitting it for publishing consideration, corresponding with the editor, and preparing the final revision. Learning is one of the functions of the process—as much for the author as for the intended readership. Willingness to understand the complexity of publishing and the rules associated with different phases of the process should enhance an author's success in placing manuscripts.

There are many professional activities other than authorial ones through which educators can contribute to the vitality of their field; among them are the advisory services related to publishing, including membership in committees that oversee publication and on editorial boards of journals and service in refereeing manuscripts. Professional service as an advisor to an editor or publisher is a critical activity requiring informed attention. Maintaining publications' health is of fundamental importance in view of the role they play for authors and the field. I urge involvement.

From discussions with colleagues, I have learned that publishing is perceived as operating in a "black box". Potential and actual authors do not know enough about the process to ask good questions. Professional associations and institutions should include in their agendas activities that address communication in education. The current literature on publishing and the experience of persons in all areas of education can assist others not only to understand publishing but also to grapple with the issues related to this area of professional activity.

This book has been written to foster greater autonomy among readers who want their writings to contribute to the dialogue in education. Its success will be measured by the readers' experiences and their assumptions of professional obligation.

Appendix A
GUIDES TO JOURNALS IN EDUCATION

There are numerous guides to journals in the field of education. They vary in their degrees of specialization, national versus international orientation, and currency of information.

Described below are three guides that list journals in all fields, including education, and two guides that focus on education journals. Uncited will be those references that are relevant only to specific areas within education.

General Guides

The readers of this book will gain the most pertinent information from the *Directory of Publishing Opportunities in Journals and Periodicals,* 4th ed. (Chicago: Marquis Academic Media, Marquis Who's Who, Inc., 1979). This volume treats over 3,400 specialized and professional journals, with over 200 of them in education in general, educational administration, and elementary, secondary, and higher education. The foreign entries accept manuscripts written in English. For this and the guides to be described, I will not list all of the items included in each journal's profile but will select some of general and special interest.

Each journal profile gives the address and telephone number of the publisher (and the editor if different), date of origin, frequency of publication, number of articles in each issue, and price. It names the editor and managing editor, briefly describes the contents and purposes of the periodical, the topics covered, and the audience to whom it is addressed. The profile identifies such manuscript requirements as style, length, number of copies to submit, the need for an abstract, and information regarding payments.

In addition, the journal's position on simultaneous submission is given, along with copyright and reprint information, and whether a letter to the editor should precede submission. There is also information on the disposition of manuscripts—whether a submission is acknowledged, the average lengths of time to reach a decision on acceptance and from acceptance to publication, whether rejected manuscripts are returned and if so, whether they are accompanied by criticism.

Many more periodicals, including journals, are listed in *Ulrich's International Periodicals Directory,* 19th ed. (New York: R. R. Bowker Co., 1980). This standard directory covering over 62,000 periodicals is now being revised yearly. It has a large "education" section that is separated into education in general, adult education, higher education, international education programs, school organization and administration, special education and rehabilitation, and teaching methods and curriculum.

The profiles are very brief and include basic identifying material such as the country of origin, the publisher's name and address, the editor's name, the year founded, frequency of publication, price, and where indexed.

The third general guide containing information on education journals is *The Standard Periodical Directory,* 7th ed., 1980-82 (New York: Oxbridge Publications, 1980). It profiles over 66,600 periodicals published in North America. Except for school administration, most education journals are not distinguished by specialty. It also provides information about college and alumni magazines in a separate section.

This directory is distinguished by its identification of the names of many persons active in each journal's editorial office, information on advertising rates and production, and the distribution of readership.

Education Journal Guides

Two guides were published in 1975 by Scarecrow Press (Metuchen, N.J.): a *Guide to Periodicals in Education and its Academic Disciplines* by W. Camp and B. Schwark, and *Education/Psychology Journals: A Scholar's Guide* by D. Arnold and K. Doyle, Jr.

The former lists 602 United States education and education-related periodicals. The profiles contain basic information, such as circulation, names and addresses, a statement of editorial policy, the number of articles in each issue, whether unsolicited material is welcome, and if book reviews are published. There is information on manuscript preparation, the time factors after the receipt of a paper, and whether critiques accompany the returned work.

Scarecrow's second entry contains "detailed descriptions of 122 journals of professional interest to many psychologists, education-ists, educational psychologists, and educators" (p. v). It focuses on the psychology-education linkage, and in addition to basic infor-mation, each profile has special features of interest to scholars. Examined are such items as typical content areas of articles, the disciplines and specialties of readers and contributors, intended audience, criteria and procedures for manuscript acceptance or rejection, information on refereeing, time frames, and if manu-scripts are published in order of acceptance.

The guides noted here provide useful information. Familiarity with their content in addition to a critical understanding of a journal's recent publishing history should provide a sufficient foundation for successful manuscript placement.

Appendix B
SAMPLE MANUSCRIPT REVIEW FORM

An editor interested in a variety of inquiry modes will either specify them and their elements or be less detailed in order for the variety to be accommodated under general principles. The form on the following pages tells the referee that the journal expects to receive manuscripts having different purposes, each providing different review factors.

Some editors are more explicitly instructive by developing referee guides as opposed to reaction forms. Such guides might contain a statement of editorial objectives, the characteristics of acceptable and conditionally acceptable manuscripts, and the problems that should lead to a recommendation either for major revision or rejection. In addition, space could be available for the reviewer to record the names of other possible reviewers whose advice should prove useful to the editor and other journals that are likely to be interested in the paper should the present one decline to use it.

As stated earlier, and it cannot be repeated often enough, one can know an editor, his or her relation with referees, and what they consider knowledge worth publishing by examining their primary communication channel.

JHE

THE JOURNAL OF HIGHER EDUCATION

Ohio State University Press
2070 Neil Avenue, Columbus, Ohio 43210

READER REPORT

Title: Date sent:

A. Please evaluate the attached manuscript on the following criteria:
    (A) Excellent, (B) Good, (C) Fair, (D) Poor.

   <u>Form</u>   <u>Content</u>

   _____ Writing style and readability   _____ Originality of topic/approach

   _____ Logical development   _____ Significance of subject

   _____ Appropriate length   _____ Significance to <u>JHE</u> readers

   _____ Appropriateness of Author's stated objectives to treatment as defined below.

B. Please comment on the paper based on the appropriate form of inquiry used. Some
    criteria specific to the modes of inquiry are noted. Authors will receive your
    remarks which should address both strengths and weaknesses and contain suggestions.

    1. As a <u>research</u> paper--use of theory and the available literature, design,
        sampling, data gathering procedures, treatment and interpretation of data,
        importance of results, practical and substantive implications, use of
        tables and graphs.

    2. As a <u>technical</u> paper--grounding in the state of the product development art,
        appropriate product development procedures, adequate field testing and
        evaluation, factors of cost, feasibility, and adaptability.

    3. As a <u>professional practice</u> paper--defensible description of problem and its
        context, explicitness of assumptions, delineation of alternatives and defence
        of chosen course of action with practical/theoretical implications.

    4. As a <u>literature</u> review-- comprehensiveness, coherence, impartiality, development
        of meanings for practitioner, suggested needed scholarship.

    5. As a <u>policy</u> paper--use of explicit frame of reference with decision-making
        potential, definitions of elements of analysis, explicit criteria to assess
        alternatives, grounded predictions and their relation to ideal consequences.

<u>Comments for the author</u>:

Published in affiliation with the American Association for Higher Education

C. Comments for Editor's eyes only:

Recommendation:

Accept _____

Reject _____

Revise _____

_____

Reader

Appendix C
PUBLISHER'S AGREEMENT

A publisher's agreement is reproduced on the opposite page. It is written in clear English, and it protects both the author and the publisher throughout an article's publishing history. Page 2, not reproduced, provides space for signatures.

JE

THE JOURNAL OF HIGHER EDUCATION

Ohio State University Press
2070 Neil Avenue, Columbus, Ohio 43210

AGREEMENT between

the Ohio State University Press and the Author

of the Article at present titled

which has been accepted for publication in the <u>Journal of Higher Education</u>.

<u>Grant of Rights and Agreement to Publish</u>. The Author grants and assigns exclusively to the Ohio State University Press the entire literary property and all rights of whatsoever kind in the Article, and every part thereof, now or hereafter protected by the copyright laws of the United States, for the period of copyright provided by law, and of all foreign countries in all languages, and agrees that the copyright may be taken and held in the name of the Ohio State University Press. Among the rights so granted and assigned are the right of first publication of the Article in the Journal, the right to reproduce the Article in subsequent editions of that issue of the Journal of which the Article is a part, the right to reproduce the Article separately, and the right to make assignments of subsidiary rights to republish or reprint, in any reproduced form, the Article in whole, part, condensation, and translation.

The Ohio State University Press, in turn, grants to the Author the right of republica-tion of the Article in any book of which he is author or editor, subject only to his giving appropriate credit in the book, in a form to be specified in writing by the Ohio State University Press, to original publication of the Article in the Journal and to the Ohio State University Press.

The Ohio State University Press will undertake to publish, at the earliest practicable time, the Article as a part of an issue of the Journal.

<u>Warranty, Previous Publication, and Previous Registration</u>. The Author warrants that he is the author of the Article, except of those passages that are clearly identified as quotations, and has the sole and exclusive right to make this Agreement. The Author guarantees that the Article has not been previously published or registered with the United States Copyright Office (if it has been so registered, the date of registration is _____).

<u>Indemnity</u>. The Author warrants that the Article is without matter that is libelous or otherwise injurious, or that infringes any proprietary right or copyright, and that he will hold the Ohio State University Press harmless from any claim, suit, or pro-ceeding instituted by reason of publication of the Article and alleging any violation or breach by the Author of the representations, agreements, or grants contained in this Agreement.

<u>Proofreading, Reprints, and Complimentary Copies</u>. The Ohio State University Press will give the Author an opportunity to read and correct galley proof of the Article. The Author agrees to assume responsibility for the accuracy of the galley proof and to reimburse the Ohio State University Press for any alterations, other than correc-tions of errors made by the typesetter, whose costs are in excess of five percent of the total cost of typesetting the Article. The Author agrees that if he fails to return the galley proof by the date set by the Ohio State University Press, production and publication of the Article may proceed without his approval.

The Ohio State University Press will give the Author an opportunity to order reprints of the Article and will provide the Author with two complimentary copies of the Journal issue in which the Article is printed.

<u>Subsidiary Rights and Compensation</u>. The Ohio State University Press will attempt to obtain the Author's approval of any requests received for permission to reprint or to translate all or any portion of the Article to be published in a book. Should a fee be charged for this use of the Article, and should the fee amount to more than $20.00. all monies will be divided equally between the Author and the Ohio State University Press.

Appendix D
THE BOOK REVIEW

Although we have concentrated on the publication of article manuscripts, brief mention should be made regarding the development of book reviews.

The Rules

Journal editors or their designates usually select reviewers for books received or requested from publishers. A person interested in reviewing new releases should communicate his or her *specific* interests to the editor or book review editor if one is noted on the masthead.

It cannot be overemphasized that one's chances of being selected are improved if one's interests are clearly detailed. For example, an author may be an expert on desegregation, but the editor must know if this expertise is supported by a background in demography, law, or ethics—among other possibilities.

Submitting a sample of one's published work as a reviewer may also improve one's chances. Editors are cautious when inviting new reviewers to treat important books, and opportunities to break into the review network are enhanced if the editor is confident of an author's judgment and writing ability.

Although editors receive unsolicited reviews of current books and might very well accept them, it is not recommended that authors write reviews without prior indication that they will be considered. Timing is an important consideration. Book review editors typically request a review shortly after a volume is in their hands, which is often before the book is made available to the general public. Regardless of the quality of an unsolicited review received after the commissioned one, the editor will abide by the initial commitment—unless the original review is beyond repair.

Authors interested in reviewing should place their names on the mailing lists of appropriate publishers and periodically consult *Publishers Weekly* to develop an awareness of anticipated releases.

The Book Review

In his classic essay "What is a Good Review?," Joseph Wood Krutch (1937) observes, "Of all literary forms the book review is the one most widely cultivated and least often esteemed" (p. 456). It is "the most difficult of all forms of literary criticism" because the writer has many things to accomplish in a very short space.

Editors' instructions to reviewers reflect their expectations and the goals of their journals. Thus, a research journal review should concentrate on a book's contribution to the field, while the association journal is interested in its contribution to reader interest. Nevertheless, it is likely that Krutch's three minimum tasks will be asked of reviewers: to describe the book, to discuss its quality, and to judge the volume.

It is unnecessary for these tasks, or the ones included on the review form below, to be accomplished in order. Nor do the chapters or sections of the book demand serial treatment, with equal space devoted to each.

Readers are judging the reviewer as much as they are interested in his or her reactions. Insight, care, objectivity, balance, empathy, depth, and breadth are among the attributes that readers expect in a review. An incredible review tells the reader much about the reviewer's credibility and complexity of thought.

Regardless of its eventual use, writers claim that the development of a review while reading a book promotes a high level of comprehension. This additional outcome from reviewing might be the most important.

THE JOURNAL OF HIGHER EDUCATION

Ohio State University Press
2070 Neil Avenue, Columbus, Ohio 43210

On behalf of the Editorial Board of the <u>Journal of Higher Education</u>, I am pleased to invite your participation as a reviewer of the following book:

The review should be between 800 to 1,000 words in length, and we would appreciate receiving it by

It is our belief that a review should accomplish the following objectives (adapted from the guidelines for <u>Sociology: Reviews of New Books</u>):

1. <u>Describe the book's content</u>. About half of the review should describe the content of the book and the orientation of the author.

2. <u>Evaluate contribution to knowledge and practice</u>. The review should address the book's strong and weak points as they relate to its contribution to scholarship and its implications for practice.

3. <u>Provide comparison with other works</u>. The review should place the book in context with other works addressing a similar theme and suggest how the new volume contributes to the literature base.

4. <u>Indicate the intended audience</u>. The review should suggest, briefly, who is likely to benefit from the book, given the author's approach and the assumptions made about readers' previous knowledge of the subject. While not appropriate for all books, the quality of the volume as a product--edited, manufactured--if extraordinarily high or low, might allow for comment.

We are enclosing a return-mail envelope for your reply. If you are able to accept the assignment, the book will be sent to you immediately.

Thank you very much for your consideration of this request.

Very sincerely,

Robert J. Silverman
Editor

RJS/kah

Published in affiliation with the American Association for Higher Education

BIBLIOGRAPHY

Argyris, C. *Intervention theory and method: A behavioral science view.* Reading, Massachusetts: Addison-Wesley Publishing Co., 1970.

Agryris, C. *The applicability of organizational sociology.* New York: Cambridge University Press, 1972.

Agryris, C. & Schon, D.A. Theory in practice: Increasing professional effectiveness. San Francisco: Jossey-Bass, 1974.

Bennis, W. Thoughts from a victim of "info-overload anxiety" *Antioch Review,* 1977, 35, 158-167.

Biglan, A. The characteristics of subject matter in different academic areas. *Journal of Applied Psychology,* 1973, 57(3), 195-203. (a)

Biglan, A. Relationship between subject matter characteristics and the structure and output of university departments. *Journal of Applied Psychology,* 1973, 57(3), 204-213. (b)

Crane, D. *Invisible colleges: Diffusion of knowledge in scientific communities.* Chicago: University of Chicago Press, 1972.

Dixon, B. Telling the people: Science in the public press since the Second World War. In A. J. Meadows (Ed.), *Development of science publishing in Europe.* Amsterdam: Elsevier Science Publishers, 1980.

Ewing, D. W. *Writing for results: In business, government, and the professions.* New York: Wiley-Interscience, 1974.

Farago, P.. *Science and the media.* London: Oxford University Press, 1976.

Johnston, D. F. *Copyright Handbook.* New York: R. R. Bowker Co., 1978.

Krutch, J. W. What is a good review? *The Nation,* April 17, 1937. Reprinted in A. L. Bader & C. F. Wells (Eds.), *Essays of three decades.* New York: Harper & Bros, 1939, pp. 456-458.

Lewis, G. L. Paradigms, consensus, and group structure: A comparison of three scientific subfields. Unpublished manuscript, University of Pittsburgh, 1975.

Mahoney, M. J. *Scientist as subject: The psychological imperative.* Cambridge, Massachusetts: Ballinger Publishing Co., 1976.

Mitroff, I. I., & Kilmann, R. H. *Methodological approaches to social science.* San Francisco: Jossey-Bass, 1978.

Mueller, R. K. Leading-edge-leadership. *Human Systems Management,* 1980, 1(1), 17-27.

Nagi, S. Z., & Corwin, R. G. (Eds.). *The social contexts of research.* New York: John Wiley & Sons, 1972.

101

Nisbet, J., & Broadfoot, P. *The impact of research on policy and practice in education* ʾberdeen, Scotland: The University Press, Aberdeen, 1980.

Rothman, J. *Using research in organizations: A guide to successful application.* Beverly Hills, California: Sage Publications, 1980.

Schubert, W. H. Recalibrating educational research: Toward a focus on practice. *Educational Researcher,* 1980, *9*(1), 17-24.

Shaver, J. P., & Norton, R. S. Randomness and replication in ten years of the *American Educational Research Journal. Educational Researcher,* 1980, *9*(1), 9-15.

Silverman, R. J. Editor-field relationships: The accountability of education journal gatekeepers. American Society for Information Science Fifth Mid-year Meeting, Nashville, May 22, 1976. Published in *Proceedings,* Washington, D.C. 1976. (a)

Silverman, R. J. The education editor as futurist. *Teachers College Record,* 1976, *77*(4), 473-493. (b)

Silverman, R. J. The education journal editor: A portrait. *Journal of Education,* 1976, 158(4), 39-68. (c)

Silverman, R. J. Diffusion of educational knowledge through journals: Gate-keepers' selection criteria. *Viewpoints in Teaching and Learning,* 1978, *54*(2), 1-22.

Silverman, R. J. Commitments of editors in education. *The Educational Forum,* 1980, *44*(2), 231-242.

Smart, J. C., & Elton, C. F. Goal orientation of academic departments: A test of Biglans's model. *Journal of Applied Psychology,* 1975, *60*(5), 580-588.

Smart, J. C., & McLaughlin, G. W. Reward structures of academic disciplines. *Research in Higher Education,* 1978, *8*(1), 39-55.

Susman, G. L., & Evered, R. D. An assessment of the scientific merits of action research. *Administrative Science Quarterly,* 1978, *23*(4), 582-603.

Thatcher, S. G. *What publishers need to know about the new copyright law: A synopsis for practical use.* New York: American University Press Services, Inc., for the Association of American University Presses, Inc. 1977.

Ward, A. W, Hall, B. W., & Schramm, C. F. Evaluation of published educational research: A national survey. *American Educational Research Journal,* 1975, *12*(2), 109-128.

Weiss, C. H. Knowledge creep and decision accretion. *Knowledge: Creation, Diffusion, Utilization,* 1980, *1*(3), 381-404. (a)

Weiss, C. H. with Bucuvalas, M. J. Social science research and decision-making. New York: Columbia University Press, 1980. (b)

Wilson, P. *Public knowledge, private ignorance: Toward a library and information policy.* Westport, Connecticut: Greenwood Press, 1977.

INDEX

A

Abstract, 73
Acceptance of manuscript, 53-54, 71-77
Accountability, 46, 58
Artwork, 73-74
Authors
    experienced, 47
    new, 47
    treatment of institutions, 83-84
Authorship of manuscript, 83

B

Backlog of manuscripts, 37, 77
Bibliography, 101-102
Book review, 98-100

C

Call for manuscripts, 9, 28
Charges, 39, 74, 86-87
Circulation, 23, 38
Citations
    by authors, 85-86
    by others, 23
Complimentary copies, 76
Contract, 76, 86-88, 96-97
Copy editing, 35, 40, 74-75
Copyright, 76, 86-88
Criteria for acceptance
    process, 59, 61
    content, 59, 62
    by journal type
        association, 67-68
        professional, 66-67
        research, 63-64
        scholarly, 64-66

D

Delays
    in publishing, 8
    in reviewing, 38-39, 42, 45, 54
Disciplinary knowledge, 5-8, 10, 24-25

E

Editor bias, 6, 25, 39, 44, 47, 52
Editors, education journals
    association, 31-32
    professional, 29-31
    research, 25-26
    scholarly, 27-29
    responsiveness, in general, 54
Editorial board
    see Referees
Editorial response, 53-54
Education as a field, 6, 23, 24, 26
    27, 29, 33
Education journals
    association, 31-32
    identifying type, 32-33
    professional, 29-31
    research, 24-26
    scholarly, 26-29
Education research
    dysfunctions, 26, 65-66
    quality, 11
    use of, 11-12, 14-15, 63, 65

F

Footnote use, 72-73
Form letter, 49

G

Guides to journals in education, 89-91